ROSICRUCIAN DAWN

The three foundational texts
that announced the
Rosicrucian Brotherhood

FAMA FRATERNITATIS

CONFESSIO FRATERNITATIS

THE CHYMICAL MARRIAGE OF CHRISTIAN ROSENCREUTZ.

Preface, Introduction and Translation
A.E.WAITE

British Library Cataloguing in Publication Data

A catalogue record for this book is available from the British Library

ISBN-13: 978-1-913751-20-3

Cover Illustration: *Mons Philosophorum*.
Steffan Michelspacher (1616)

Back Cover: *Dat Rosa Mel Apibus*
('The rose gives honey to the bees')
Johann Thedore deBry (d. 1598).

CONTENTS

ILLUSTRATIONS

The Jewel of the Rose Croix. J. Augustus Knapp

The Pelican was said to wound itself to feed its young
- hence its association with the Redeemer.

ROSICRUCIAN

DAWN

PREFACE.

Beneath the broad tide of human history there flow the stealthy undercurrents of the secret societies, which frequently determine in the depths the changes that take place upon the surface. These societies have existed in all ages and among all nations, and tradition has invariably ascribed to them the possession of important knowledge in the religious scientific or political order according to the various character of their pretensions. The mystery which encompasses them has invested them with a magical glamour and charm that to some extent will account for the extravagant growth of legend about the Ancient Mysteries, the Templars, the Freemasons, and the Rosicrucians, above all, who were the most singular in the nature of their ostensible claims and in the uncertainty which envelopes them.

"A halo of poetic splendour," says Heckethorn,[1] "surrounds the Order of the Rosicrucians; the magic lights of fancy play round their graceful day-dreams, while the mystery in which they shrouded themselves lends additional attraction to their history. But their brilliancy was that of a meteor. It just flashed across the realms of imagination and intellect, and vanished for ever; not, however, without leaving behind some permanent and lovely traces of its hasty passage. . . . Poetry and romance are deeply indebted to the Rosicrucians for many a fascinating creation. The literature of every European country contains hundreds of pleasing fictions, whose machinery has been borrowed from their system of philosophy, though that itself has passed away."

The facts and documents concerning the Fraternity of the Rose Cross, or of the Golden and Rosy Cross, as it is called by Sigmund Richter,[2] are absolutely unknown to English readers. Even well-informed people will learn with astonishment the extent and variety of the Rosicrucian literature which hitherto has lain buried in rare pamphlets, written in the old German tongue, and in the Latin commentaries of the later alchemists. The stray gleams of casual information which may be gleaned from popular encyclopædias cannot be said to convey any real knowledge, while the essay of Thomas De Quincey on the "Rosicrucians and Freemasons," though valuable as the work of a sovereign prince of English prose composition, is a mere transcript from an exploded German savant, whose facts are tortured in the interests of a somewhat arbitrary hypothesis. The only writer in this country who claims to have treated the subject seriously and at length is Hargrave Jennings, who, in "The Rosicrucians, their Rites and Mysteries," &c., comes forward as the historian of the Order. This book, however, so far from affording any information on the questions it professes to deal with, "keeps guard over" [3] the secrets of the Fraternity, and is

---

1. 'Secret Societies of all Ages and Countries'.
2. Die Warhaffte and vollkommene, Bereitung des Philosophischen Steins, der Bruderschafft aus dem Orden des Gulden-und-Rosen Creutzes. 1710.
3. "No student of occult philosophy need fear that we shall most carefully keep guard - standing sentry (so to speak) over those other and more recondite systems which are connected with our subject."

6

simply a mass of ill-digested erudition concerning Phallicism and Fire-Worship, the Round Towers of Ireland and Serpent Symbolism, offered with a charlatanic assumption of secret knowledge as an exposition of Rosicrucian philosophy.[4]

The profound interest now manifested in all branches of mysticism, the tendency, in particular, of many cultured minds towards those metaphysical conceptions which are at the base of the alchemical system, the very general suspicion that other secrets than that of manufacturing gold are to be found in the Pandora's Box of Hermetic and Rosicrucian allegories,[5] make it evident that the time has come to collect the mass of material which exists for the elucidation of this curious problem of European history, and to depict the mysterious Brotherhood as they are revealed in their own manifestos and in the writings of those men who were directly or indirectly in connection with them. Such a publication will take the subject out of the hands of unqualified writers, and of the self-constituted pontiffs of darkness and mystery who trade upon the ignorance and curiosity of their readers.

As the result of conscientious researches, I have succeeded in discovering several tracts and manuscripts in the Library of the British Museum, whose existence, so far as I am aware, has been unknown to previous investigators, while others, including different copies and accounts of the "Universal Reformation," as well as original editions of the "Chymical Marriage of Christian Rosy Cross," which are not in the Library Catalogue, though less generally obscure, I have met with in a long series of German pamphlets belonging to the first quarter of the seventeenth century. These, with all other important and available facts and documents, I have carefully collected and now publish them in the present volume, either summarised or in extenso according to their value, and I offer for the first time in the literature of the subject the Rosicrucians represented by themselves. I claim that I have performed my task in a sympathetic but impartial manner, purged from the bias of any particular theory, and above all uncontaminated by the pretension to superior knowledge, which claimants have never been able to substantiate.

---

4. In reviewing an enlarged edition of this work, published in 1879, the Westminster Review remarks: "In the 'Rosicrucians' we have come across perhaps the most absurd book that it has ever been our fortune to review. . . . And through the whole runs a very unwholesome undercurrent."–W. R. N. S., vol. lvi. p. 256.

5. On this point see "A Suggestive Inquiry into the Hermetic Mystery and Alchemy," published anonymously in the year 1850, in London, and Hitchock's "Remarks on Alchemy," also anonymous, New York, 1865.

INTRODUCTION

In cruce sub sphera venit sapientia vera – Hermetic Axiom.

La rose qui a été de tout temps l'emblême de la beauté, de la vie, de l'amour et du plaisir, exprimait mystiquement toutes les protestations manifestées à la renaissance. . . . Rénuir la rose, à la croix, tel était le problème posé par la Haute Initiation. – Éliphas Lévi.

Three derivations are offered of the name Rosicrucian. The first, which is certainly the most obvious, deduces it from the ostensible founder of the order, Christian Rosenkreuze. I shall show, however, that the history of this personage is evidently mythical or allegorical, and therefore this explanation merely takes the inquiry a step backward to the question, What is the etymology of Rosenkreuze? The second derivation proposed is from the Latin words Ros, dew, and Crux, cross. This has been countenanced by Mosheim, who is followed by *Ree's Encyclopædia*; and other publications. The argument in its favour may be fairly represented by the following quotation:– "Of all natural bodies, dew was deemed the most powerful dissolvent of gold; and the cross, in chemical language, was equivalent to light; because the figure of a cross exhibits at the same time the three letters of which the word lux, or light, is compounded. Now, lux is called . . . the seed or menstruum of the red dragon, or, in other words, that gross and corporeal light, which, when properly digested and modified, produces gold. Hence it follows, if this etymology be admitted, that a Rosycrucian philosopher is one who by the intervention and assistance of the dew, seeks for light, or, in other words, the substance called the Philosopher's Stone." [1]

This opinion exaggerates the importance attributed to the dew of the alchemists. The universal dissolvent has figured under various names, of which ros is by no means most general; the comprehensive "*Lexicon Alchymiæ*" does not mention it. According to Gaston le Doux, in his "*Dictionnaire Hermétique*," Dew, simply so called, signifies Mercury; Dew of the Philosophers is the matter of the stone when under the manipulation of the artist, and chiefly during its circulations in the philosophical egg. The White and Celestial Dew of the Wise is the philosophical stone perfected to the White. Mosheim derived his opinion from Peter Gassendi,[2] and from a writer in Eusebius Renandot's "*Conferences Publiques*," [3] who confesses that he knew nothing whatsoever of the Rosicrucians till the task of speaking on the subject was imposed on him by the Bureau d'Addresse. He says:–"Dew, the most powerful dissolvent of gold which is to be found among natural and non-corrosive substances, is nothing else but light coagulated and rendered corporeal; when it is artistically concocted and digested in its own vessel during a suitable period it is the true menstruum of the Red

Dragon, i.e., of gold, the true matter of the Philosophers. The society desiring to bequeath to posterity the ineffaceable sign of this secret, caused them to adopt the name Frères de la Rozée Cuite." The mystic triad of the Society, F. R. C., has been accordingly interpreted Fratres Roris Cocti, the Brotherhood of the Concocted or Exalted Dew, but the explanation has little probability in itself.

"Several chemists," says Pernetz, in his "*Dictionnaire Mytho-Hermétique*," "have regarded the dew of May and September as the matter of the Magnum Opus, influenced doubtless by the opinion of various authors that dew was the reservoir of the universal spirit of Nature. . . . But when we seriously study the texts of the true philosophers, wherein they make reference to dew, we are soon convinced that they only speak of it by a similitude, and that theirs is metallic, that is, it is the mercurial water sublimated into vapour within the vase, and precipitated at the bottom in the form of fine rain. Thus when they write of the dew of the month of May, they are referring to that of their philosophic Spring, which is governed by the gemini of the alchemical Zodiack, which differs from the ordinary astronomical Zodiack. Philalethes has positively said that their dew is their mercurial water rising from putrefaction."

The third derivation is that which was generally adopted, even from the beginning, by writers directly or indirectly connected with the Rosicrucians. It deduces the term in question from the words rosa, rose, and crux. This is sanctioned by various editions of the society's authoritative documents, which characterise it as the Broederschafft des Roosen Creutzes, that is, the Rose-Crucians, or Fratres Rosatæ Crucis, according to the "*Confessio Recepta*," terms quite excluding the conception of dew, which in German is Thau, while in Latin the Brothers of the Dewy Cross would be Fratres Roratæ Crucis. This derivation is also supported by the supposed symbol of the Order, whose "emblem, monogram, or jewel," says Godfrey Higgins, "is a Red Rose on a Cross, thus:–

When it can be done it is surmounted with a glory and placed on a calvary. When it is worn appended and made of cornelian, garnet, ruby, or red glass, the calvary and glory are generally omitted." [4]

Mr Hargrave Jennings, who borrows the whole of this passage[5] without acknowledgment of any kind, also tells us that "the jewel of the Rosicrucians is formed of a transparent red stone with a red cross on one side and a red rose on the other–thus it is a crucified rose."

All derivations, however, are to some extent doubtful and tentative. The official proclamations of the Society are contained in the *"Fama Fraternitatis,"* and in the *"Confessio Fraternitatis,"* which, in their original editions, appear to describe it simply as the Fraternitas de R. C., while the initials of its founder are given as C. R. *"The Chemical Nuptials of Christian Rosen Kreuze,"* published anonymously at Strasbourg in 1616, and undeniably connected with the order, seem to identify it as the Brotherhood of the Rose-Cross, and its founder as Father Rosycross. These designations at any rate were immediately adopted in Germany, and they appear in the subsequent editions of both manifestos, though as early as 1618 I find Michael Maier, the alchemist, expressing a different opinion on this point in his *"Themis Aurea, hoc est, De Legibus Fraternitatis R. C. Tractatus."* "No long time elapsed, when the Society first became known by that which was written, before an interpreter came forward who conjectured those letters to signify the Rose Cross, in which opinion the matter remains till this present, notwithstanding that the Brothers in subsequent writings do affirm it to be erroneously so denominated, and testify that the letters R. C. denote the name of their first inaugurator.[6] If the mind of one man could search that of another and behold formed therein the idea or sensible and intelligible form, there would be no necessity for speech or writing among men. But this being denied to us while we subsist in this corporeal nature, though doubtless granted to pure intelligences, we explain our rational conceptions one to another by the symbols of language and writing. Therefore letters are of high efficacy when they embrace a whole society and maintain order therein, nor is an opportunity afforded to the curious to draw omens from integral names, nor from families situations, nor from places, persons, nor from persons the secrets of affairs."

Proposing his own definitions, he says:–"I am no augur nor prophet, notwithstanding that once I partook of the laurel, and reposed a few brief hours in the shadow of Parnassus; nevertheless, if I err not, I have unfolded the significance of the characters R. C. in the enigmas of the sixth book of the Symbols of the Golden Table. R signifies Pegasus, and C, if the sense not the sound be considered, lilium. Let the KNOWLEDGE OF THE ARCANA be the key to thee. Lo, I give thee the Arcanum! *d. wmml. zii. w. sgqqhka. x.* Open if thou canst. . . . Is not this the hoof of the Red Lion or the drops of the Hippocrene fountain?" Beneath this barbarous jargon we discern, however, an analogy with the Rose symbolism. Classical tradition informs us that the Red Rose sprang from the blood of Adonis, but Pegasus was a winged horse which sprang from the blood of Medusa, and the fountain of Hippocrene was produced by a stroke of the hoof of Pegasus.

In England the pseudonymous author of the *"Summum Bonum,"* who is supposed to be Robert Fludd, gives a purely religious explanation of the Rose Cross symbol, asserting it to mean "the Cross sprinkled with the rosy blood of

Christ."[7] The general concensus of opinion is preferable to fanciful interpretations, and we may therefore safely take the words Rosa and Crux as explanatory of the name Rosicrucian, and by Fratres R. C. we may understand Fratres Roseæ Crucis, despite the silence of the manifestos and the protests of individual alchemists.

The next question which occurs is the significance of this curious emblem – a Red Rose affixed to a red, or, according to some authors, a golden cross. This question cannot be definitely answered. The characteristic sign of a secret society will be naturally as mysterious as itself in the special meaning which the society may attach to it, but some intelligence concerning it can perhaps be gleaned from its analysis with universal symbolism. Now, the Rose and the Cross, in their separate significance, are emblems of the most palmary importance and the highest antiquity.

There is a Silver Rose, called Tamara Pua, in the Paradise of the Brahmans. "This Paradise is a garden in heaven, to which celestial spirits are first admitted on their ascent from the terrestrial sphere. The Rose contains the images of two women, as bright and fair as a pearl; but these two are only one, though appearing as if distinct according to the medium, celestial or terrestrial, through which they are viewed. In the first aspect she is called the Lady of the Mouth, in the other, the Lady of the Tongue, or the Spirit of Tongues. In the centre of this Silver Rose, God has his permanent residence."

A correspondence will be readily recognised between this divine woman or virgin – two and yet one, who seems to typify the Logos, the Spirit of Wisdom, and the Spirit of Truth – and the two-edged sword of the Spirit in the Apocalypse, the *Sapientia quæ ex ore Altissimii prodiit*, as it is called in the sublime Advent antiphon of the Latin Church. The mystical Rose in the centre of the allegorical garden is continually met with in legend. Buddha is said to have been crucified for robbing a garden of a flower,[8] and after a common fashion of mythology, the divine Avatar of the Indians is henceforth identified with the object for which he suffered, and he becomes himself "a flower, a Rose, a Padma, Lotus, or Lily." Thus he is the Rose crucified, and we must look to the far East for the origin of the Rosicrucian emblem. According to Godfrey Higgins, this is "the Rose of Isuren, of Tamul, and of Sharon, crucified for the salvation of men – crucified," he continues, "in the heavens at the vernal equinox." In this connection we may remember the Gnostic legend that Christ was crucified in the Empyrean; and as Nazareth, according to St Jerome, signified the flower, and was situated in Carmel, "the vineyard or garden of God," Jesus of Nazareth, by a common extension of the symbolism, is sometimes identified as this crucified flower.[9]

In classical fable, the garden of Midas, the King of the Phrygians, was situated at the foot of Mount Bermion, and was glorified by the presence of roses with sixty petals, which exhaled an extraordinary fragrance. Now, the rose was sacred to Dionysius, or Bacchus, and Bacchus endowed Midas with the power of transmuting everything into gold; so here is a direct connection between the Rose and Alchemy.

In the *Metamorphoses of Apuleius*, Lucius is restored to his human shape by devouring a chaplet of roses. Everywhere the same typology meets us. The Peruvian Eve sinned by plucking roses, which are also called Frute del Arbor.[10] A messenger from heaven announces to the Mexican Eve that she will bear a Son who shall bruise the serpent's head; he presents her with a Rose, and this gift was followed by an Age of Roses, as in India there was the Age of the Lotus.

There are occasional allusions to the Rose in the Hebrew Scriptures, but it is used as a poetic image rather than an arcane symbol, and as such it has been always in high favour with poets. [11]

In the west it appears for the first time in allegorical literature as the central figure in the "four-square garden" of the ancient "Romance of the Rose." The first part of this poem was written by Guillaume de Lorris before the year 1260, and it was completed by Jean de Meung, whose death occurred in the year 1316, according to the general opinion. This extraordinary work, once of universal popularity, is supposed by some of its commentators to admit of an alchemical interpretation, and openly professes the principles of the Magnum Opus.[12] The garden, or vergier, which contains the Rose, is richly sculptured on its outer walls with symbolical figures of Hatred, Treason, Meanness, Covetousness, Avarice, Envy, Sadness, Age, Hypocrisy, Poverty – all the vices and miseries of mortality. Idleness opens the gate to him, Merriment greets him and draws him into the dance, and then he beholds the God of Love, accompanied by Dous-Regars, a youth who carries his bows and arrows, by Beauty, Wealth, Bounty, Frankness, Courtesy, &c. The lover, while he is contemplating the loveliness of the Rose,

> *Qui est si vermeille et si fine . . .*
> *Des foilles i ot quatre paire,*
> *Que Nature par grand mestire*
> *I ot assises tire à tire.*
> *Le coe ot droite comme jons,*
> *Et par dessus siet li boutons,*
> *Si qu 'il ne cline ne ne pent.*
> *L' odor de lui entor s' espent;*
> *La soatisme qui en ist,*
> *Toute la place replenist,* [13]

is pierced by the shafts of the deity, but he does not in spite of his sufferings abandon his project, which is to possess the Rose, and after imprisonment and various adventures,

> *La conclusion du Rommant*
> *Est que vous voyez cy l'Amant*

Qui prent la Rose à son plaisir,
En qui estoit tout son désir.

It will require no acquaintance with the methods of the symbolists to discern the significance of this allegory:–

La Rose c'est d'Amour le guerdon gracieux.[14]

But a little later the same emblem reappears in the sublime poem of Dante. The Paradise of the *Divina Commedia* consists, says Eliphas Lévi, of "a series of Kabbalistic circles divided by a Cross, like Ezekiel's pantacle; a Rose blossoms in the centre of this Cross, and it is for the first time that we find the symbol of the Rosicrucians publicly and almost categorically revealed."

The passage referred to, so far as regards the Rose, is as follows:–

There is in heaven a light, whose goodly shine
Makes the Creator visible to all
Created, that in seeing him alone
Have peace; and in a circle spreads so far,
That the circumference were too loose a zone
To girdle in the sun. All is one beam,
Reflected from the summit of the first,
That moves, which being hence and vigour takes.
And as some cliff; that from the bottom eyes
His image mirror'd in the crystal flood,
As if to admire his brave apparelling
Of verdure and of flowers; so, round about,
Eyeing the light, on more than million thrones,
Stood, eminent, whatever from our earth
Has to the skies return'd. How wide the leaves
Extended to their utmost, of this ROSE,
Whose lowest step embosoms such a space
Of ample radiance! Yet, nor amplitude
Nor height impeded, but my view with ease
Took in the full dimension of that joy.
Near or remote, what then avails, where God
Immediate rules,[15] *and Nature, awed, suspends*
Her sway? Into the yellow of the Rose
Perennial, which, in bright expansiveness,
Lays forth its gradual blooming, redolent
Of praises to the never-wintering sun. . . .
Beatrice led me. . . .
In fashion as a snow-white Rose lay then
Before my view the saintly multitude,

Which in his own blood Christ espoused. Meanwhile
That other host that soar aloft to gaze
And celebrate His glory whom they love,
Hovered around, and like a troop of bees
Amid the vernal sweets alighting now,
Now clustering where their fragrant labour glows,
Flew downward to the mighty flower; a rose
From the redundant petals streaming back
Unto the steadfast dwelling of their joy.
Faces had they of flame, and wings of gold:
The rest was whiter than the driven snow.
And as they flitted down into the flower,
From range to range fanning their plumy loins,
Whispered the peace and ardour which they won
From that soft winnowing. Shadow none, the vast
Interposition of such numerous flights
Cast from above, upon the flower, or view
Obstructed aught. For through the Universe
Wherever merited, Celestial Light
Glides freely, and no obstacle prevents.

CARY'S DANTE, *The Paradise*, xxx., xxxi.

"Not without astonishment will it be discovered," continues Lévi, "that the *Roman de la Rose* and the *Divine Comedy* are two opposite forms of the same work – initiation into intellectual independence, satire on all contemporary institutions and allegorical formulations of the great secrets of the Rosicrucian Society. These important manifestations of occultism coincide with the epoch of the downfall of the Templars, since Jean de Meung or Clopinel, contemporary of Dante's old age, flourished during his most brilliant years at the Court of Philippe le Bel. The 'Romance of the Rose' is the epic of ancient France. It is a profound work in a trivial guise, as learned an exposition of the mysteries of occultism as that of Apuleius. The Rose of Flamel, of Jean de Meung, and of Dante, blossomed on the same rose-tree."

This is ingenious and interesting, but it assumes the point in question, namely, the antiquity of the Rosicrucian Fraternity, which, it is needless to say, cannot be proved by the mere existence of their symbols in the mystical poetry of a remote period. In the Paradise of Dante we find, however, the emblem whose history we are tracing, placed, and assuredly not without reason, in the supreme, central heaven amidst the intolerable manifestation of the Untreated Light, the Shecinah of Rabbinical theosophy,[16] the chosen habitation of God – "a sacred Rose and Flower of Light, brighter than a million suns, immaculate, inaccessible, vast, fiery

14

with magnificence, and surrounding God as if with a million veils. This symbolic Rose is as common a hierogram throughout the vast temples and palaces of the Ancient East as it is in the immense ruins of Central America." [17]

From the time of the Guelphs and the Ghibellines a common device in heraldry is the Rose-Emblem. It figures on our English coins; it is used as a royal badge in the Civil War between the houses of York and Lancaster, it is associated above all with the great mediæval cultus of the Mother of God, being our Lady's flower *par excellence*, as the lily is characteristic of St Joseph. "As an emblem of the Virgin, the Rose, both white and red, appears at a very early period; it was especially so recognised by St Dominic, when he instituted the devotion of the rosary, with direct reference to St Mary. The prayers appear to have been symbolised as roses." [18] In Scandinavia the same flower was sacred to the goddess Holda, who is called "Frau Rosa," and "it was partly transferred, as were other emblems of Holda, Freyja, and Venus, to the Madonna, who is frequently called by the Germans, Mariën-Röschen ... But there has been a tendency to associate the White Rose with the Virgin Mary, that being chiefly chosen for her feast-days, while the more earthly feelings associated with the 'Frau Rosa,' are still represented in the superstitions connected with the Red Rose."

In Germany it appears as the symbol of silence. It was sculptured on the ceiling of the banquet hall to warn the guests against the repetition of what was heard beneath it. "The White Rose was especially sacred to silence. It was carved in the centre of the Refectory of the ancients for the same reason," and the expression *Sub Rosa*, which was equivalent among the Romans to an inviolable pledge, originated in the ancient dedication of the flower to Aphrodite, and its reconsecration by Cupid to Harpocrates, the tutelary deity of Silence, to induce him to conceal the amours of the goddess of love.

In mediæval alchemy Rosa signifies Tartarum, and in the twelfth Clavis of Basil Valentine there is a vase or yoni with a pointed lingam rising from its centre, and having on each side a sprig surmounted by a Rose. Above is the well-known emblem ☿ which symbolises the accomplishment of the *Magnum Opus*, while through an open window the sun and moon shed down their benign influence and concur in the consummation of the ineffable act.[19]

The same Rose-symbol is to be found in the hieroglyphics of Nicholas Flamel –

> *The mystic Rose*
> *Of Hermic lore, which issues bright and fair,*
> *Strange virtues circling with the sap therein,*
> *Beneath the Universal Spirit's breath,*
> *From the Mercurial Stone.*

Finally, in 1598, Henry Khunrath, a supreme alchemical adept, published his *Amphitheatrum Sapientiæ Æternæ*, containing nine singular pantacles, of which the fifth is a Rose of Light, in whose centre there is a human form extending its arms in the form of a cross, and thus reversing the order.

The Cross is a hierogram of, if possible, still higher antiquity than the floral emblem. It is at any rate more universal and contains a loftier and more arcane significance. Its earliest form is the Crux Ansata, ☿

which, according to some authorities, signified hidden wisdom, and the life of the world to come; according to others, it is the lingam; as the hieroglyphic sign of Venus it is an ancient allegorical figure, and represents the metal copper in alchemical typology. The Crux Ansata and the Tau T

are met with on most Egyptian monuments. In the latter form it was an emblem of the creative and generative energy, and, according to Payne Knight, was, even in pre-Christian times, a sign of salvation.

The Cross, "the symbol of symbols," was used also by the Chaldæans; by the Phoenicians, who placed it on their coins; by the Mexicans, who paid honour to it and represented their God of the Air, nailed and immolated thereon; by the Peruvians, who, in a sacred chamber of their palace, kept and venerated a splendid specimen carved from a single piece of fine jasper or marble; and by the British Druids. It was emblazoned on the banners of Egypt, and in that country, as in China, was used to indicate "a land of corn and plenty." When divided into four equal segments it symbolised the primeval abode of man, the traditional Paradise of Eden. It entered into the monograms of Osiris, of Jupiter Ammon, and of Saturn; the Christians subsequently adopted it, and the Labarum of Constantine is identical with the device of Osiris. It is equally common in India, and, according to Colonel Wilford, is exactly the Cross of the Manichees, with leaves, flowers, and fruits springing from it. It is called the divine tree, the tree of the gods, the tree of life and knowledge, and is productive of all things good and desirable.[20]

According to Godfrey Higgins we must go to the Buddhists for the origin of the Cross, "and to the Lama of Thibet, who takes his name from the Cross, called in his language Lamh." The Jamba, or cosmic tree, which Wilford calls, the tree of life and knowledge, figures in their maps of the "world as a cross 84 joganas (answering to the 84 years of the life of Him who was exalted upon the Cross), or 423 miles high, including the three steps of the Calvary, with which, after the orthodox Catholic fashion, it was invariably represented. The neophyte of the Indian Initiations was sanctified by the sign of a Cross, which was marked on every part of his body. After his perfect regeneration it was again set upon ⊥ his forehead and inverted ⊥ upon his breast." [21]

The paschal lamb of the Jewish passover was roasted on a cross-shaped wooden spit, and with this sign Ezekiel ordered the people to be marked who were to be spared by the destroyer. Thus it figures as a symbol of salvation, but classical mythology attributes its invention to Ixion, who was its first victim. As an instrument of suffering and death, it is not, however, to be found on ancient monuments. It had no orthodox shape among the Romans when applied to this purpose, and the victims were either tied or nailed, "being usually left to perish by thirst and hunger." [22]

In the Christendom of both the East and West this divine symbol has a history too generally known to need recapitulation here. On this point the student may consult the *Dictionary of Christian Antiquities*, where a mass of information is collected.

The following interesting passage will show the connection which exists between the Cross and alchemy. "In common chemistry," says Pernetz, crosses form characters which indicate the crucible, vinegar, and distilled vinegar. But as regards hermetic science, the Cross is ... the symbol of the four elements. And as the philosophical stone is composed of the most pure substance of the grosser elements ..., they have said, *In cruce salus*, salvation is in the Cross; by comparison with the salvation of our souls purchased by the blood of Jesus Christ who hung on the tree of the Cross. Some of them have even pushed their audacity further, and fear not to employ the terms of the New Testament to form their allegories and enigmas. Jean de Roquetaillade, known under the name of Jean de Rupe Scissa, and Arnaud de Villeneuve, say in their works on the composition of the Stone of the Philosophers:– It is needful that the Son of Man be lifted up on the Cross before being glorified; to signify the volatilisation of the fixed and igneous part of the matter." [23]

I have briefly traced the typological history of the Rose and Cross. It is obvious, as I have already remarked, that the antiquity of these emblems is no proof of the antiquity of a society which we find to be using them at a period subsequent to the Renaissance. It does not even suppose that society's initiation into the hieratic secrets which the elder world may have summarised in those particular symbols. In the case which is in question, such a knowledge would involve the antiquity of the Rosicrucians, because it is only at a time long subsequent to their first public appearance that the past has been sufficiently disentombed to uncover the significance of its symbols to uninitiated students. Can a correspondence be established between the meaning of the Rose and the Cross as they are used by the ancient hierogrammatists, and that of the Rose-Cross as it is used by the Rosicrucian Fraternity? This is the point to be ascertained. If a connection there be, then in some way, we may not know what, the secret has been handed down from generation to generation, and the mysterious brotherhood which manifested its existence spontaneously at the beginning of the seventeenth century, is affiliated with the hierophants of Egypt and India, who, almost in the night of time, devised their allegories and emblems for the blind veneration of the vulgar and as lights to those who knew.

In the fifth book of the *Histoire de la Magie*, Eliphas Lévi provides the following commentary on the Rosicrucian symbol:–

"The Rose, which from time immemorial has been the symbol of beauty and life, of love and pleasure, expressed in a mystical manner all the protestations of the Renaissance. It was the flesh revolting against the oppression of the spirit, it was Nature declaring herself to be, like grace, the daughter of God, it was love refusing to be stifled by the celibate, it was life desiring to be no longer barren, it was humanity aspiring to a natural religion, full of love and reason, founded on the revelation of the harmonies of existence of which the Rose was for initiates the living and blooming symbol. The Rose, in fact, is a pantacle; its form is circular, the leaves of the corolla are heart-shaped, and are supported harmoniously by one another; its colour presents the most delicate shades of primitive hues; its calyx is purple and gold. . . . The conquest of the Rose was the problem offered by initiation to science, while religion toiled to prepare and establish the universal, exclusive, and definitive triumph of the Cross.

"The reunion of the Rose and the Cross, such was the problem proposed by supreme initiation, and, in effect, occult philosophy, being the universal synthesis, should take into account all the phenomena of Being."

This extremely suggestive explanation has the characteristic ingenuity of the hierophants of theosophical science, but it has no application whatsoever to the ostensible or ascertainable aims of the Rosicrucian adepts. It is the product of intellectual subtlety and the poetic gift of discerning curious analogies; it is quite beside the purpose of serious historical inquiry, and my object in quoting it here is to show by the mere fact of its existence that the whole question of the significance of the Crucified Rose, in its connection with the society, is one of pure conjecture, that no Rosicrucian manifestos and no acknowledged Brother have ever given any explanation concerning it, and that no presumption is afforded by the fact of its adoption for the antiquity of the society or for its connection with universal symbolism.

The researches of various writers, all more or less competent, have definitely established the *Crux Ansata* as typical of the male and female generative organs in the act of union, the Egyptian Tau, with its variants as typical of the masculine potency, and the Rose as the feminine emblem. Then by a natural typological evolution the Cross came to signify the divine creative energy which fecundated the obscure matrix of the primeval substance and caused it to bring forth the universe.

The simple union of the Rose and the Cross suggests the same meaning as the *Crux Ansata*, but the crucified Buddhistic Rose may be a symbol of the asceticism which destroys natural desire. There is little correspondence, in either case, with known Rosicrucian tenets, and, therefore, the device of the Rose-Cross is separated from ancient symbolism, and is either a purely arbitrary and thus unexplainable sign, or its significance is to be sought elsewhere.

Now, I purpose to show that the Rosicrucians were united with a movement, which, originating in Germany, was destined to revolutionise the world of thought and to transform the face of Europe; that the symbols of the Rose and the Cross were prominently and curiously connected with this movement, and that the subsequent choice of these emblems by the secret society in question, followed naturally from the fact of this connection, and is easily explainable thereby. To accomplish this task satisfactorily, I must first lay before my readers the facts and documents which I have collected concerning the Fraternity. [24]

Footnotes

1. Mosheim, Book iv., sect. 1.

2. "Examen Philosophiæ Fluddanæ," sect. 15, op. iii,, 261.

3. "Conferences du Bureau d'Addresse," vol. v., p. 509.

4. Anacalypsis, ii., p. 243.

5. "The Rosicrucians," &c., p. 281. Ed. 1870.

6. The "Fama Fraternitatis" makes use of the initials C. R., afterwards of R. C., C. R. C., &c., to designate their founder.

7. Elsewhere he interprets the letters F.R.C. to mean Faith, Religion, and Charity. See Renandot, "Conferences Publiques," v., p. 509.

8. The same story is told of Indra, who was crucified by the keepers of the Hindoo Paradise for having robbed it.

9. Professor Max Müller considers the word ῥόδον to be Aryan, and originally to have meant simply a sprig or flower.

10. "Mexican Antiquities," vol. vi., p. 120.

11. In Persia it is connected with the nightingale. "Tradition says that the bird utters a plaintive cry whenever the flower is gathered, and that it will hover round the plant in the spring-time, till, overpowered with its fragrance, it falls senseless to the ground. The Rose is supposed to burst forth from its bud at the opening song of the nightingale. You may place a handful of fragrant herbs p. 13 and flowers before the nightingale," say the Persian poets. "Yet he wishes not, in his constant and faithful heart, for more than the sweet breath of his beloved Rose."–Friend, "Flowers and Flower Lore." There is a Persian Feast of Roses, which lasts the whole time the flower is in bloom.

12. See in particular the verses 16914 to 16997, and the speech of Genius.

"Jean de Meung," says Langlet du Fresnoy in his "Histoire de la Philosophie Hermétique," flourished at the Court and at Paris in the pontificate of John XXII., and according to the fashion of the times was addicted to the curious sciences, and in particular to Hermetic Philosophy. He composed two treatises called "Nature's Remonstrances to the Alchemist," and "The Alchemist's Answer to Nature."

13.   *Amongs the knoppes I these one*
     So faire, that of the remnant none
     Ne preise I halfe so well as it,
     Whan I avise in my wit,
     For it so well was enlumined
     With colour red, as well fined
     As nature could it make faire,
     And it hath leaves well foure paire,
     That kinde hath set through his knowing
     About the red roses springing,
     The stalke was as rishe right,
     And thereon stood the knoppe upright.
     That it ne bowed upon no side,
     The swote smell sprung so wide,
     That it died all the place about.

CHAUCER, 'The Romaunt of the Rose.'

14. Baïf–"Sonnet to Charles IX."

15. Compare the Oriental legend, previously cited, of that Silver Rose in which God has His permanent residence. It is an extraordinary instance of identity in the celestial symbolism of East and West.

16. See Additional Notes, No. 1.

17. "The Book of God," part iii., p. 511.

18. Hilderic Friend, "Flowers and Flower-Lore."

19. See Additional Notes, No. 2.

20. "Asiatic Researches," x. 124. The pre-Christian cross is not infrequently associated with a tree or trees. Balfour, "Cyclop. of India," i., p. 891.

21. "History of Initiations."

22. Higgins' "Anacalypsis," i., pp. 500, 503.

23. "Dictionnaire Mytho-Hermétique."

24. For further details of the antecedents of the Rosicrucian fraternity, see *The Real History of the Rosicrucians*, A. E. Waite, 1887.

Allgemeine vnd General

REFORMATION,

der gantzen weiten Welt.

Beneben der

FAMA FRA

TERNITATIS,

Deß Löblichen Ordens des
Rosenkreutzes / an alle Gelehrte
vnd Häupter Europæ geschrie-
ben:

Auch, einer kurtzen RESPONSION
von dem Herrn Haselmeyer gestellet / welcher
deßwegen von den Jesuitern ist gefänglich ein-
gezogen / vnd auff eine Galleren ge-
schmiedet:

Itzo öffentlich in Druck verfertiget
vnd allen trewen Hertzen communiciret
worden.

❧❧❧ ❧❧❧ ❧❧❧ ❧❧❧ ❧❧❧ ❧❧❧

Gedruckt zu Cassel/ durch Wilhelm Wessell/

ANNO M. DC, XIV.

THE FAMA FRATERNITATIS OF THE MERITORIOUS
ORDER OF THE ROSY CROSS,

ADDRESSED TO THE LEARNED IN GENERAL,
AND THE GOVERNORS OF EUROPE.

The original edition of the 'Universal Reformation' contained the manifesto bearing the above title, but which the notary Haselmeyer declares to have existed in manuscript as early as the year 1610, as would also appear from a passage in the Cassel edition of 1614, the earliest which I have been able to trace. It was reprinted with the *Confessio Fraternitatis* and the *Allgemeine Reformation der Ganzen Welt* at Franckfurt-on-the-Mayne in 1615. A Dutch translation was also published in this year, and by 1617 there had been four Frankfurt editions, the last omitting the 'Universal Reformation,' which, though it received an elaborate alchemical elucidation by Brotoffer,[1] seems gradually to have dropped out of notice. "Other editions," says Buhle, "followed in the years immediately succeeding, but these it is unnecessary to notice. In the title-page of the third Frankfurt edition stands – *First printed at Cassel in the year 1616.* But the four first words apply to the original edition, the four last to this.[2]

FAMA FRATERNITATIS

or a Discovery of the Fraternity of the
Most Laudable Order of the Rosy Cross

Seeing the only wise and merciful God in these latter days hath poured out so richly His mercy and goodness to mankind, whereby we do attain more and more to the perfect knowledge of His Son Jesus Christ and of Nature, that justly we may boast of the happy time wherein there is not only discovered unto us the half part of the world, which was heretofore unknown and hidden, but He hath also made manifest unto us many wonderful and never-heretofore seen works and creatures of Nature, and, moreover, hath raised men, indued with great wisdom, which might partly renew and reduce all arts (in this our spotted and imperfect age) to perfection, so that finally man might thereby understand his own nobleness and worth, and why he is called *Microcosmos*, and how far his knowledge extendeth in Nature.

Although the rude world herewith will be but little pleased, but rather smile and scoff thereat; also the pride and covetousness of the learned is so great, it will not suffer them to agree together; but were they united, they might, out of all those things which in this our age God doth so richly bestow on us, collect *Librum Naturæ*, or, a Perfect Method of all Arts. But such is their opposition that they still keep, and are loth to leave, the old course, esteeming Porphyry, Aristotle, and Galen, yea, and that which hath but a meer show of learning, more than the clear and manifested Light and Truth. Those, if they were now living, with much joy would leave their erroneous doctrines; but here is too great weakness for such a great work. And although in Theologie, Physic, and the Mathematic, the truth doth oppose it itself, nevertheless, the old Enemy, by his subtilty and craft, doth shew himself in hindering every good purpose by his instruments and contentious wavering people.

To such an intention of a general reformation, the most godly and highly-illuminated Father, our Brother, C. R. C., a German, the chief and original of our Fraternity, hath much and long time laboured, who, by reason of his poverty (although descended of noble parents), in the fifth year of his age was placed in a cloyster, where he had learned indifferently the Greek and Latin tongues, and (upon his earnest desire and request), being yet in his growing years, was associated to a Brother, P. A. L., who had determined to go to the Holy Land. Although this Brothers dyed in Ciprus, and so never came to Jerusalem, yet our Brother C. R. C. did not return, but shipped himself over, and went to Damasco, minding from thence to go to Jerusalem. But by reason of the feebleness of his body he remained still there, and by his skill in physic he obtained much favour with the Turks, and in the meantime he became acquainted with the Wise Men of Damcar in Arabia, and beheld what great wonders they wrought, and how Nature was discovered unto them.

Hereby was that high and noble spirit of Brother C. R. C. so stired up, that Jerusalem was not so much now in his mind as Damasco;[3] also he could not bridle his desires any longer, but made a bargain with the Arabians that they should carry him for a certain sum of money to Damcar.

He was but of the age of sixteen years when he came thither, yet of a strong Dutch constitution. There the Wise Men received him not as a stranger (as he himself witnesseth), but as one whom they had long expected; they called him by his name, and shewed him other secrets out of his cloyster, whereat he could not but mightily wonder.

He learned there better the Arabian tongue, se that the year following he translated the book M into good Latin, which he afterwards brought with him. This is the place where he did learn his Physick and his Mathematics, whereof the world hath much cause to rejoice, if there were more love and less envy.

After three years he returned again with good consent, shipped himself over *Sinus Arabicus* into Egypt, where he remained not long, but only took better notice there of the plants and creatures. He sailed over the whole Mediterranean Sea for to come unto Fez, where the Arabians had directed him.

It is a great shame unto us that wise men, so far remote the one, from the other, should not only be of one opinion, hating all contentious writings, but also be so willing and ready, under the seal of secresy, to impart their secrets to others. Every year the Arabians and Africans do send one to another, inquiring one of another out of their arts, if happily they had found out some better things, or if experience had weakened their reasons. Yearly there came something to light whereby the Mathematics, Physic, and Magic (for in those are they of Fez most skilful) were amended. There is now-a-days no want of learned men in Germany, Magicians, Cabalists, Physicians, and Philosophers, were there but more love and kindness among them, or that the most part of them would not keep their secrets close only to themselves.

At Fez he did get acquaintance with those which are commonly called the Elementary inhabitants, who revealed unto him many of their secrets, as we Germans likewise might gather together many things if there were the like unity and desire of searching out secrets amongst us.

Of these of Fez he often did confess, that their Magia was not altogether pure, and also that their Cabala was defiled with their Religion; but, notwithstanding, he knew how to make good use of the same, and found still more better grounds for his faith, altogether agreeable with the harmony of the whole world, and wonderfully impressed in all periods of time. Thence proceedeth that fair Concord, that as in every several kernel is contained a whole good tree or fruit, so likewise is included in the little body of man, the whole great world, whose religion, policy, health, members, nature, language, words, and works, are agreeing, sympathizing, and in equal tune and melody with God, Heaven, and Earth; and that which is disagreeing with them is error, falsehood, and of the devil, who alone is the first, middle, and last cause of strife, blindness, and darkness in the world. Also, might one examine all and several persons upon the earth, he should find that which is good and right is always agreeing with itself, but all the rest is spotted with a thousand erroneous conceits.

After two years Brother R. C. departed the city Fez, and sailed with many costly things into Spain, hoping well, as he himself had so well and profitably spent his time in his travel, that the learned in Europe would highly rejoyce with him, and begin to rule and order all their studies according to those sure and sound foundations. He therefore conferred with the learned in Spain, shewing unto them the errors of our arts, and how they might be corrected, and from whence they should gather the true *Inditia* of the times to come, and wherein they ought to agree with those things that are past; also how the faults of the Church and the whole *Philosophia Moralis* were to be amended. He shewed them new growths, new fruits, and beasts, which did concord with old philosophy, and prescribed them new Axiomata, whereby all things might fully be restored. But it was to them a laughing matter, and being a new thing unto them, they feared that their great name would be lessened if they should now again begin to learn, and acknowledge their many years' errors, to which they were accustomed, and wherewith they had gained them enough. Who so loveth unquietness, let him be reformed (they said). The same song was also sung to him by other nations, the which moved him the more because it happened to him contrary to his expectation, being then ready bountifully to impart all his arts and secrets to the learned, if they would have but undertaken to write the true and infallible Axiomata, out of all faculties, sciences, and arts, and whole nature, as that which he knew would direct them, like a globe or circle, to the onely middle point and centrum, and (as it is usual among the Arabians) it should onely serve to the wise and learned for a rule, that also there might be a society in Europe which might have gold, silver, and precious stones, sufficient for to bestow them on kings for their necessary uses and lawful purposes, with which [society] such as be governors might be brought up for to learn all that which God hath suffered man to know, and thereby to be enabled in all times of need to give their counsel unto those that seek it, like the Heathen Oracles.

Verily we must confess that the world in those days was already big with those great commotions, labouring to be delivered of them, and did bring forth painful, worthy men, who brake with all force through darkness and barbarism, and left us who succeeded to follow them. Assuredly they have been the uppermost point in *Trygono igneo*, whose flame now should be more and more brighter, and shall undoubtedly give to the world the last light.

Such a one likewise hath Theophrastus been in vocation and callings, although he was none of our Fraternity, yet, nevertheless hath he diligently read over the Book M, whereby his sharp ingenium was exalted; but this man was also hindered in his course by the multitude of the learned and wise-seeming men, that he was never able peaceably to confer with others of the knowledge and understanding he had of Nature. And therefore in his writings he rather mocked these busie bodies, and doth not shew them altogether what he was; yet, nevertheless, there is found with him well grounded the afore-named Harmonia, which without doubt he had imparted to the learned, if he had not found them rather worthy of subtil vexation then to be instructed in greater arts and sciences. He thus with a free and careless life lost his time, and left unto the world their foolish pleasures.

But that we do not forget our loving Father, Brother C. R., he after many painful travels, and his fruitless true instructions, returned again into Germany, the which he heartily loved, by reason of the alterations which were shortly to come, and of the strange and dangerous contentions. There, although he could have bragged with his art, but specially of the transmutations of metals, yet did he esteem more Heaven, and men, the citizens thereof, than all vain glory and pomp.

Nevertheless, he built a fitting and neat habitation, in the which he ruminated his voyage and philosophy, and reduced them together in a true memorial. In this house he spent a great time in the mathematics, and made many fine instruments, *ex omnibus hujus artis partibus*, whereof there is but little remaining to us, as hereafter you shall understand.

After five years came again into his mind the wished for Reformation; and in regard [of it] he doubted of the ayd and help of others, although he himself was painful, lusty, and unwearisom; howsoever he undertook, with some few adjoyned with him, to attempt the same. Wherefore he desired to that end to have out of his first cloyster (to the which he bare a great affection) three of his brethren, Brother G. V., Brother I. A., and Brother I. O., who had some mere knowledge of the arts than at that time many others had. He did bind those three unto himself, to be faithful, diligent, and secret, as also to commit carefully to writing all that which he should direct and instruct them in, to the end that those which were to come, and through especial revelation should be received into this Fraternity, might not be deceived of the least sillable and word.

After this manner began the Fraternity of the Rosie Cross – first, by four persons onely, and by them was made the magical language and writing, with a large dictionary, which we yet dayly use to God's praise and glory, and do finde great wisdom therein. They made also the first part of the Book M, but in respect that that labour was too heavy, and the unspeakable concourse of the sick hindred them, and also whilst his new building (called *Sancti Spiritus*) was now finished, they concluded to draw and receive yet others more into their Fraternity. To this end was chosen Brother R. C., his deceased father's brother's son; Brother B., a skilful painter; G. G., and. P. D., their secretary, all Germains except I. A., so in all they were eight in number, all batchelors and of vowed virginity, by whom was collected a book or volumn of all that which man can desire, wish, or hope for.

Although we do now freely confess that the world is much amended within an hundred years, yet we are assured that our Axiomata shall immovably remain unto the world's end, and also the world in her highest and last age shall not attain to see anything else; for our ROTA takes her beginning from that day when God spake *Fiat* and shall end when he shall speak *Pereat*; yet God's clock striketh every minute, where ours scarce striketh perfect hours. We also stedfastly beleeve, that if our Brethren and Fathers had lived in this our present and clear light, they would more roughly have handled the Pope, Mahomet, scribes, artists, and sophisters, and showed themselves more helpful, not simply with sighs and wishing of their end and consummation.

When now these eight Brethren had disposed and ordered all things in such manner, as there was not now need of any great labour, and also that every one was sufficiently instructed and able perfectly to discourse of secret and manifest philosophy, they would not remain any longer together, but, as in the beginning they had agreed, they separated themselves into several countries, because that not only their Axiomata might in secret be more profoundly examined by the learned, but that they themselves, if in some country or other they observed anything, or perceived some error, might inform one another of it.

Their agreement was this:–

First, That none of them should profess any other thing then to cure the sick, and that gratis.

Second, None of the posterity should be constrained to wear one certain kind of habit, but therein to follow the custom of the country.

Third, That every year, upon the day C., they should meet together at the house *Sancti Spiritus*, or write the cause of his absence.

Fourth, Every Brother should look about for a worthy person who, after his decease, might succeed him.

Fifth, The word R. C. should be their seal, mark, and character.

Sixth, The Fraternity should remain secret one hundred years.

These six articles they bound themselves one to another to keep; five of the Brethren departed, onely the Brethren B. and D. remained with the Father, Brother R. C., a whole year. When these likewise departed, then remained by him his cousen and Brother I. O., so that he hath all the days of his life with him two of his Brethren. And although that as yet the Church was not cleansed, nevertheless, we know that they did think of her, and what with longing desire they looked for. Every year they assembled together with joy, and made a full resolution of that which they had done. There must certainly have been great pleasure to hear truly and without invention related and rehearsed all the wonders which God hath poured out here and there throughout the world. Every one may hold it out for certain, that such persons as were sent, and joyned together by God and the Heavens, and chosen out of the wisest of men as have lived in many ages, did live together above all others in highest unity, greatest secresy, and most kindness one towards another.

After such a most laudable sort they did spend their lives, but although they were free from all diseases and pain, yet, notwithstanding, they could not live and pass their time appointed of God. The first of this Fraternity which dyed, and that in England, was I. O., as Brother C. long before had foretold him; he was very expert, and well learned in Cabala, as his Book called H witnesseth. In England he is much spoken of, and chiefly because he cured a young Earl of Norfolk of the leprosie. They had concluded, that, as much as possibly could be, their burial place should be kept secret, as at this day it is not known unto us what is become of some of them, yet every one's place was supplied with a fit successor. But this we will confesse publickly by these presents, to the honour of God, that what secret soever we have learned out of the book M, although before our eyes we behold the image and pattern of all the world, yet are there not shewn unto us our misfortunes, nor hour of death, the which only is known to God Himself, who thereby would have us keep in a continual readiness. But hereof more in our Confession, where we do set down thirty-seven reasons wherefore we now do make known our Fraternity, and proffer such high mysteries freely, without constraint and reward. Also we do promise more gold then both the Indies bring to the King of Spain, for Europe is with child, and will bring forth a strong child, who shall stand in need of a great godfather's gift.

After the death of I. O., Brother R. C. rested not, but, as soon as he could, called the rest together, and then, as we suppose, his grave was made, although hitherto we (who were the latest) did not know when our loving Father R. C. died, and had no more but the bare names of the beginners, and all their successors to us. Yet there came into our memory a secret, which, through dark and hidden words and speeches of the hundred years, Brother A., the successor of D. (who was of the last and second row of succession, and had lived amongst many of us), did impart unto us of the third row and succession; otherwise we must confess, that after the death of the said A., none of us had in any manner known anything of Brother C. R., and of his first fellow-brethren, then that which was extant of them in our philosophical BIBLIOTHECA, amongst which our AXIOMATA was held for the chiefest, ROTA MUNDI for the most artificial, and PROTHEUS for the most profitable. Likewise, we do not certainly know if these of the second row have been of like wisdom as the first, and if they were admitted to all things.

It shall be declared hereafter to the gentle reader not onely what we have heard of the burial of Brother R. C., but also it shall be made manifest publicly, by the foresight, sufferance, and commandment of God, whom we most faithfully obey, that if we shall be answered discreetly and Christian-like, we will not be ashamed to set forth publickly in print our names and surnames, our meetings, or anything else that may be required at our hands.

Now, the true and fundamental relation of the finding out of the high-illuminated man of God, Fra: C. R. C., is this:– After that A. in *Gallia Narbonensi* was deceased, there succeeded in his place our loving Brother N. N. This man, after he had repaired unto us to take the solemn oath of fidelity and secresy, informed us *bona fide*, that A. had comforted him in telling him, that this Fraternity should ere long not remain so hidden, but should be to all the whole German nation helpful, needful, and commendable, of the which he was not in anywise in his estate ashamed. The year following, after he had performed his school right, and was minded now to travel, being for that purpose sufficiently provided with Fortunatus' purse, he thought (he being a good architect) to alter something of his building, and to make it more fit. In such renewing, he lighted upon the Memorial Table, which was cast of brasse, and containeth all the names of the Brethren, with some few other things. This he would transfer into another more fitting vault, for where or when Brother R. C. died, or in what country he was buried, was by our predecessors concealed and unknown unto us. In this table stuck a great naile somewhat strong, so that when it was with force drawn out it took with it an indifferent big stone out of the thin wall or plaistering of the hidden door, and so unlooked for uncovered the door, whereat we did with joy and longing throw down the rest of the wall and cleared the door, upon which was written in great letters–

Post CXX Annos Patebo,

with the year of the Lord under it. Therefore we gave God thanks, and let it rest that same night, because first we would overlook our *Rota* – but we refer ourselves again to the Confession, for what we here publish is done for the help of those that are worthy, but to the unworthy, God willing, it will be small profit. For like as our door was after so many years wonderfully discovered, also there shall be opened a door to Europe (when the wall is removed), which already doth begin to appear, and with great desire is expected of many. In the morning following we opened the door, and there appeared to our sight a vault of seven sides and seven corners, every side five foot broad, and the height of eight foot. Although the sun never shined in this vault, nevertheless, it was enlightened with another sun, which had learned this from the sun, and was situated in the upper part in the center of the siding. In the midst, instead of a tomb-stone, was a round altar, covered with a plate of brass, and thereon this engraven:–

A. C. R. C. Hoc universi compendium unius mihi sepulchram feci.
Round about the first circle or brim stood,

Jesus mihi omnia.

In the middle were 4 figures, inclosed in circles, whose circumscription was,

1. Nequaquam Vacuum.
2. Legis Jugum.
3. Libertas Evangelii.
4. Dei Gloria Intacta.

This is all clear and bright, as also the seventh side and the two heptagons. So we kneeled down altogether, and gave thanks to the sole wise, sole mighty, and sole eternal God, who hath taught us more than all men's wits could have found out, praised be His holy name. This vault we parted in three parts, the upper part or siding, the wall or side, the ground or floor. Of the upper part you shall understand no more at this time but that it was divided according to the seven sides in the triangle which was in the bright center; but what therein is contained you (that are desirous of our Society) shall, God willing, behold the same with your own eyes. Every side or wall is parted into ten squares, every one with their several figures and sentences, as they are truly shewed and set forth *concentratum* here in our book. The bottom again is parted in the triangle, but because therein is described the power and rule of the Inferior Governors, we leave to manifest the same, for fear of the abuse by the evil and ungodly world. But those that are provided and stored with the Heavenly Antidote, do without fear or hurt, tread on and bruise the head of the old and evil serpent, which this our age is well fitted for. Every side or wall had a door for a chest, wherein there lay divers things, especially all our books, which otherwise we had, besides the *Vocabulario* of Theophrastus Paracelsus of Hohenheim, and these which daily unfalsifieth we do participate. Herein also we found his *Itinerarium* and *Vita*, whence this relation for the most part is taken. In another chest were looking-glasses of divers virtues, as also in other places were little bells, burning lamps, and chiefly wonderful artificial songs – generally all was done to that end, that if it should happen, after many hundred years, the Fraternity should come to nothing, they might by this onely vault be restored again.

Now, as we had not yet seen the dead body of our careful and wise Father, we therefore removed the altar aside; then we lifted up a strong plate of brass, and found a fair and worthy body, whole and unconsumed, as the same is here lively counterfeited,[4] with all the ornaments and attires. In his hand he held a parchment called T,[5] the which next unto the Bible is our greatest treasure, which ought not to be delivered to the censure of the world. At the end of this book standeth this following *Elogium*.

Granum pectori Jesu insitum

C. R. C. ex nobili atque splendida Germaniæ R. C. familia oriundus, vir sui seculi divinis revelationibus, subtilissimis imaginationibus, indefessis laboribus ad cœlestia atque humana mysteria; arcanavè admissus postquam suam (quam Arabico at Africano itineribus collejerat) plus quam regiam, atque imperatoriam Gazam suo seculo nondum convenientem, posteritati eruendam custodivisset et jam suarum Artium, ut et nominis, fides ac conjunctissimos heredes instituisset, mundum minutum omnibus motibus magno illi respondentem fabricasset hocque tandem preteritarum, præsentium, et futurarum, rerum compendio extracto, centenario major, non morbo (quem ipse nunquam corpore expertus erat, nunquam alios infestare sinebat) ullo pellente sed Spiritis Dei evocante, illuminatam animam (inter Fratrum amplexus et ultima oscula) fidelissimo Creatori Deo reddidisset, Pater delictissimus, Frater suavissimus, præceptor fidelissimus, amicus integerimus, a suis ad 120 annos hic absconditus est.

Underneath they had subscribed themselves,

1. *Fra.* I. A. Fra. C. H. *electione Fraternitatis caput.*

2. *Fra.* G. V. M. P. C.

3. *Fra.* F. R. C., *Junior hœres S. Spiritus.*

4. *Fra.* F. B. M. P. A., *Pictor et Architectus.*

5. *Fra.* G. G. M. P. I., *Cabalista.*

Secundi Circuli.

1. *Fra.* P. A. *Successor, Fra.* I. O., *Mathematicus.*

2. *Fra.* A. *Successor, Fra.* P. D.

3. *Fra.* R. *Successor Patris* C. R. C., *cum Christo triumphantis.*

At the end was written,

Ex Deo nascimur, in Jesu morimur, per Spiritum Sanctum reviviscimus.

At that time was already dead, Brother I. O. and Brother D., but their burial place where is it to be found? We doubt not but our Fra. Senior hath the same, and some especial thing layd in earth, and perhaps likewise hidden. We also hope that this our example will stir up others more diligently to enquire after their names (which we have therefore published), and to search for the place of their burial; the most part of them, by reason of their practice and physick, are yet known and praised among very old folks; so might perhaps our GAZA be enlarged, or, at least, be better cleared.

31

Concerning *Minutum Mundum*, we found it kept in another little altar, truly more finer then can be imagined by any understanding man, but we will leave him undescribed untill we shall be truly answered upon this our true-hearted FAMA. So we have covered it again with the plates, and set the altar thereon, shut the door and made it sure with all our seals. Moreover, by instruction, and command of our ROTA, there are come to sight some books, among which is contained M (which were made instead of household care by the praiseworthy M. P.). Finally, we departed the one from the other, and left the natural heirs in possession of our jewels. And so we do expect the answer and judgment of the learned and unlearned.

Howbeit we know after a time there will now be a general reformation, both of divine and humane things, according to our desire and the expectation of others; for it is fitting, that before the rising of the Sun there should appear and break forth Aurora, or some clearness, or divine light in the sky. And so, in the meantime, some few, which shall give their names, may joyn together, thereby to increase the number and respect of our Fraternity, and make a happy and wished for beginning of our PHILOSOPHICAL CANONS, prescribed to us by our Brother R. C., and be partakers with us of our treasures (which never can fail or be wasted) in all humility and love, to be eased of this world's labours, and not walk so blindly in the knowledge of the wonderful works of God.

But that also every Christian may know of what Religion and belief we are, we confess to have the knowledge of Jesus Christ (as the same now in these last days, and chiefly in Germany, most clear and pure is professed, and is now adays cleansed and voyd of all swerving people, hereticks, and false prophets), in certain and noted countries maintained, defended, and propagated. Also we use two Sacraments, as they are instituted with all Formes and Ceremonies of the first and renewed Church. In *Politia* we acknowledge the Roman Empire and *Quartam Monarchiam* for our Christian head, albeit we know what alterations be at hand, and would fain impart the same with all our hearts to other godly learned men, notwithstanding our handwriting which is in our hands, no man (except God alone) can make it common, nor any unworthy person is able to bereave us of it. But we shall help with secret aid this so good a cause, as God shall permit or hinder us. For our God is not blinde, as the heathen's Fortuna, but is the Churches' ornament and the honour of the Temple. Our Philosophy also is not a new invention, but as Adam after his fall hath received it, and as Moses and Solomon used it, also it ought not much to be doubted of, or contradicted by other opinions, or meanings; but seeing the truth is peaceable, brief, and always like herself in all things, and especially accorded by with *Jesus in omni parte* and all members, and as He is the true image of the Father, so is she His image, so it shal not be said, This is true according to Philosophy, but true according to Theologie; and wherein Plato, Aristotle, Pythagoras, and others did hit the mark, and wherein Enoch, Abraham, Moses, Solomon, did excel, but especially wherewith that wonderful book the Bible agreeth. All that same concurreth together, and maketh a sphere or globe whose total parts are equidistant from the center, as hereof more at large and more plain shal be spoken of in Christianly Conference (in den Boecke des Levens).

But now concerning, and chiefly in this our age, the ungodly and accursed gold-making, which hath gotten so much the upper hand, whereby under colour of it, many runagates and roguish people do use great villainies, and cozen and abuse the credit which is given them; yea, now adays men of discretion do hold the transmutation of metals to be the highest point and *fastigium* in philosophy. This is all their intent and desire, and that God would be most esteemed by them and honoured which could make great store of gold, the which with unpremeditate prayers they hope to obtain of the alknowing God and searcher of all hearts; but we by these presents publickly testifie, that the true philosophers are far of another minde, esteeming little the making of gold, which is but a *paragon*, for besides that they have a thousand better things. We say with our loving Father C. R. C., *Phy. aurium nisi quantum aurum*, for unto him the whole nature is detected; he doth not rejoice that he can make gold, and that, as saith Christ, the devils are obedient unto him, but is glad that he seeth the Heavens open, the angels of God ascending and descending, and his name written in the book of life.

Also we do testifie that, under the name of *Chymia*, many books and pictures are set forth in *Contumeliam gloriæ Dei*, as we wil name them in their due season, and wil give to the pure-hearted a catalogue or register of them. We pray all learned men to take heed of these kinde of books, for the Enemy never resteth, but soweth his weeds til a stronger one doth root them out.

So, according to the wil and meaning of Fra. C. R. C., we his brethren request again all the learned in Europe who shal read (sent forth in five languages) this our *Fama* and *Confessio*, that it would please them with good deliberation to ponder this our offer, and to examine most nearly and sharply their arts, and behold the present time with all diligence, and to declare their minde, either *communicato consilio*, or *singulatim* by print. And although at this time we make no mention either of our names or meetings, yet nevertheless every one's opinion shal assuredly come to our hands, in what language so ever it be, nor any body shal fail, whoso gives but his name, to speak with some of us, either by word of mouth, or else, if there be some lett, in writing. And this we say for a truth, that whosoever shal earnestly, and from his heart, bear affection unto us, it shal be beneficial to him in goods, body, and soul; but he that is false-hearted, or onely greedy of riches, the same first of all shal not be able in any manner of wise to hurt us, but bring himself to utter ruine and destruction. Also our building, although one hundred thousand people had very near seen and beheld the same, shal for ever remain untouched, undestroyed, and hidden to the wicked world

Sub umbra alarum tuarum, Jehova.

Footnotes

1. "Elucidarius Major, oder Ekleuchterunge über die Reformatio der ganzen Weiten Welt . . . Durch Radtichs Brotofferr." 1617.

2. De Quincey, "Rosicrucians and Freemasons."

3. Damascus and the unknown city denominated Damcar are continually confused in the German editions. Brother C. R. C. evidently did not project a journey to Damascus, which he had already reached; nevertheless this is the name appearing in this place, and I have decided on retaining it for reasons which will subsequently be made evident.

4.The illustration which is here referred to is, singularly enough, not reproduced in the text of the translation, and it is also absent from the Dutch version of 1617. As there are no other editions of the "Fama Fraternitatis" in the Library of the British Museum, I also am unable to gratify the curiosity of my readers by a copy of the original engraving.

5. In the English translation the letter I has been substituted by a typographical error, or by an error of transcription for the T which is found in all the German editions.

CONFESSIO
FRATERNITA-
TIS. R. C.

AD ERUDITOS
EUROPÆ.

Caput primum..

Uæ de noſtra Fraternitate ex Famæ R. C. clangore vobis audita ſunt, Mortales, ea nolite, vel temeraria credere, vel voluntaria ſuſpicari, JEHOVA eſt, qui mundo labaſcente, & propemodum periodo abſoluta, ad principium properante Naturæ ordinem invertit, & quæ prius fruſtia magno ſudore, indefeſſoq́ labore, quærebantur, nunc nihil tale Cogitantibus aperit, Volentibus offert, Nolentibus obtrudit: ut & Bonis ſit, quod vitæ humanæ moleſtias condiat, Inſtantiſq́ concuſſionis vehementiam frangat: Malis quod peccata, & his plagas multiplicet.

Inſtitutum noſtrum, quo optimi patris noſtri vo-

THE CONFESSIO FRATERNITATIS

The translation of this manifesto, which follows the Fama in the edition accredited by the great name of Eugenius Philalethes is prolix and careless: being made not from the Latin original but from the later German version. As a relic of English Rosicrucian literature I have wished to preserve it, and having subjected it to a searching revision throughout, it now represents the original with sufficient fidelity for all practical purposes. The "Confessio Fraternitatis" appeared in the year 1615 in a Latin work entitled "Secretioris Philosophiæ Consideratio Brevio à Philippo à Gabella, Philosophiæ studioso, conscripta; et nunc primum unà cum Confessione Fraternitatis R. C.," in lucem edita, Cassellis, excudebat G. Wesselius, a 1615, Quarto."

It was prefaced by the following advertisement:–

"Here, gentle reader, you shall finde incorporated in our Confession thirty-seven reasons of our purpose and intention, the which according to thy pleasure thou mayst seek out and compare together, considering within thyself if they be sufficient to allure thee. Verily, it requires no small pains to induce any one to believe what doth not yet appear, but when it shall be revealed in the full blaze of day, I suppose we should be ashamed of such questionings. And as we do now securely call the Pope Antichrist, which was formerly a capital offence in every place, so we know certainly that what we here keep secret we shall in the future thunder forth with uplifted voice, the which, reader, with us desire with all thy heart that it may happen most speedily.

"FRATRES R. C."

CONFESSIO FRATERNITATIS R.C.
AD ERUDITOS EUROPÆ.

CHAPTER I.

Whatsoever you have heard, O mortals, concerning our Fraternity by the trumpet sound of the Fama R. C., do not either believe it hastily, or wilfully suspect it. It is Jehovah who, seeing how the world is falling to decay, and near to its end, doth hasten it again to its beginning, inverting the course of Nature, and so what heretofore hath been sought with great pains and dayly labor He doth lay open now to those thinking of no such thing, offering it to the willing and thrusting it on the reluctant, that it may become to the good that which will smooth the troubles of human life and break the violence of unexpected blows of Fortune, but to the ungodly that which will augment their sins and their punishments.

Although we believe ourselves to have sufficiently unfolded to you in the *Fama* the nature of our order, wherein we follow the will of our most excellent father, nor can by any be suspected of heresy, nor of any attempt against the commonwealth, we hereby do condemn the East and the West (meaning the Pope and Mahomet) for their blasphemies against our Lord Jesus Christ, and offer to the chief head of the Roman Empire our prayers, secrets, and great treasures of gold. Yet we have thought good for the sake of the learned to add somewhat more to this, and make a better explanation, if there be anything too deep, hidden, and set down over dark, in the Fama, or for certain reasons altogether omitted, whereby we hope the learned will be more addicted unto us, and easier to approve our counsel.

CHAPTER II.

Concerning the amendment of philosophy, we have (as much as at this present is needful) declared that the same is altogether weak and faulty; nay, whilst many (I know not how) alledge that she is sound and strong, to us it is certain that she fetches her last breath.

But as commonly even in the same place where there breaketh forth a new disease, nature discovereth a remedy against the same, so amidst so many infirmities of philosophy there do appear the right means, and unto our Fatherland sufficiently offered, whereby she may become sound again, and new or renovated may appear to a renovated world.

No other philosophy we have than that which is the head of all the faculties, sciences, and arts, the which (if we behold our age) containeth much of Theology and Medicine, but little of Jurisprudence; which searcheth heaven and earth with exquisite analysis, or, to speak briefly thereof, which doth sufficiently manifest the Microsmus man, whereof if some of the more orderly in the number of the learned shall respond to our fraternal invitation, they shall find among us far other and greater wonders then those they heretofore did believe, marvel at, and profess.

CHAPTER III.

Wherefore, to declare briefly our meaning hereof, it becomes us to labor carefully that the surprise of our challenge may be taken from you, to shew plainly that such secrets are not lightly esteemed by us, and not to spread an opinion abroad among the vulgar that the story concerning them is a foolish thing. For it is not absurd to suppose many are overwhelmed with the conflict of thought which is occasioned by our unhoped graciousness, unto whom (as yet) be unknown the wonders of the sixth age, or who, by reason of the course of the world, esteem the things to come like unto the present, and, hindered by the obstacles of their age, live no otherwise in the world then as men blind, who, in the light of noon, discern nothing onely by feeling.

CHAPTER IV.

Now concerning the first part, we hold that the meditations of our Christian father on all subjects which from the creation of the world have been invented, brought forth, and propagated by human ingenuity, through God's revelation, or through the service of Angels or spirits, or through the sagacity of understanding, or through the experience of long observation, are so great, that if all books should perish, and by God's almighty sufferance all writings and all learning should be lost, yet posterity will be able thereby to lay a new foundation of sciences, and to erect a new citadel of truth; the which perhaps would not be so hard to do as if one should begin to pull down and destroy the old, ruinous building, then enlarge the fore-court, afterwards bring light into the private chambers, and then change the doors, staples, and other things according to our intention.

Therefore, it must not be expected that new comers shall attain at once all our weighty secrets. They must proceed step by step from the smaller to the greater, and must not be retarded by difficulties.

Wherefore should we not freely acquiesce in the onely truth then seek through so many windings and labyrinths, if onely it had pleased God to lighten unto us the sixth Candelabrum? Were it not sufficient for us to fear neither hunger, poverty, diseases, nor age? Were it not an excellent thing to live always so as if you had lived from the beginning of the world, and should still live to the end thereof? So to live in one place that neither the people which dwel beyond the Ganges could hide anything, nor those which live in Peru might be able to keep secret their counsels from thee? So to read in one onely book as to discern, understand, and remember whatsoever in all other books (which heretofore have been, are now, and hereafter shal come out) hath been, is, and shal be learned out of them? So to sing or to play that instead of stony rocks you could draw pearls, instead of wild beasts spirits, and instead of Pluto you could soften the mighty princes of the world? O mortals, diverse is the counsel of God and your convenience, Who hath decreed at this time to encrease and enlarge the number of our Fraternity, the which we with such joy have undertaken, as we have heretofore obtained this great treasure without our merits, yea, without any hope or expectation; the same we purpose with such fidelity to put in practice, that neither compassion nor pity for our own children (which some of us in the Fraternity have) shal move us, since we know that these unhoped for good things cannot be inherited, nor be conferred promiscuously.

CHAPTER V.

If there be any body now which on the other side wil complain of our discretion, that we offer our treasures so freely and indiscriminately, and do not rather regard more the godly, wise, or princely persons then the common people, with him we are in no wise angry (for the accusation is not without moment), but withall we affirm that we have by no means made common property of our arcana, albeit they resound in five languages within the ears of the vulgar, both because, as we well know, they will not move gross wits, and because the worth of those who shal be accepted into our Fraternity will not be measured by their curiosity, but by the rule and pattern of our revelations. A thousand times the unworthy may clamour, a thousand times may present themselves, yet God hath commanded our ears that they should hear none of them, and hath so compassed us about with His clouds that unto us, His servants, no violence can be done; wherefore now no longer are we beheld by human eyes, unless they have received strength borrowed from the eagle.

For the rest, it hath been necessary that the Fama should be set forth in everyone's mother tongue, lest those should not be defrauded of the knowledge thereof; whom (although they be unlearned) God hath not excluded from the happiness of this Fraternity, which is divided into degrees; as those which dwell in Damcar, who have a far different politick order from the other Arabians; for there do govern onely understanding men, who, by the king's permission, make particular laws, according unto which example the government shall also be instituted in Europe (according to the description set down by our Christianly

Father), when that shal come to pass which must precede, when our Trumpet shall resound with full voice and with no prevarications of meaning, when, namely, those things of which a few now whisper and darken with enigmas, shall openly fill the earth, even as after many secret chafings of pious people against the pope's tyranny, and after timid reproof, he with great violence and by a great onset was cast down from his seat and abundantly trodden under foot, whose final fall is reserved for an age when he shall be torn in pieces with nails, and a final groan shall end his ass's braying, the which, as we know, is already manifest to many learned men in Germany, as their tokens and secret congratulations bear witness.

CHAPTER VI.

We could here relate and declare what all the time from the year 1378 (when our Christian father was born) till now hath happened, what alterations he hath seen in the world these one hundred and six years of his life, what he left after his happy death to be attempted by our Fathers and by us, but brevity, which we do observe, will not permit at this present to make rehearsal of it; it is enough for those which do not despise our declaration to have touched upon it, thereby to prepare the way for their more close union and association with us. Truly, to whom it is permitted to behold, read, and thenceforward teach himself those great characters which the Lord God hath inscribed upon the world's mechanism, and which He repeats through the mutations of Empires, such an one is already ours, though as yet unknown to himself; and as we know he will not neglect our invitation, so, in like manner, we abjure all deceit, for we promise that no man's uprightness and hopes shall deceive him who shall make himself known to us under the seal of secresy and desire our familiarity. But to the false and to impostors, and to those who seek other things then wisdom, we witness by these presents publikely, we cannot be betrayed unto them to our hurt, nor be known to them without the will of God, but they shall certainly be partakers of that terrible commination spoken of in our Fama, and their impious designs shall fall back upon their own heads, while our treasures shall remain untouched, till the Lion shall arise and exact them as his right, receive and imploy them for the establishment of his kingdom.

CHAPTER VII.

One thing should here, O mortals, be established by us, that God hath decreed to the world before her end, which presently thereupon shall ensue, an influx of truth, light, and grandeur, such as he commanded should accompany Adam from Paradise and sweeten the misery of man: Wherefore there shall cease all falshood, darkness, and bondage, which little by little, with the great globe's revolution, hath crept into the arts, works, and governments of men, darkening the greater part of them. Thence hath proceeded that innumerable diversity of persuasions, falsities, and heresies, which makes choice difficult to the wisest men, seeing on the one part they were hindered by the reputation of philosophers and on the other by the facts of experience, which if (as we trust) it can be once removed, and instead thereof a single and self-same rule be instituted, then there will indeed remain thanks unto them which have taken pains therein, but the sum of the so great work shall be attributed to the blessedness of our age. As we now confess that many high intelligences by their writings will be a great furtherance unto this Reformation which is to come, so do we by no means arrogate to ourselves this glory, as if such a work were onely imposed on us, but we testify with our Saviour Christ, that sooner shall the stones rise up and offer their service, then there shall be any want of executors of God's counsel.

CHAPTER VIII.

God, indeed, hath already sent messengers which should testifie His will, to wit, some new stars which have appeared in *Serpentarius* and *Cygnus*, the which powerful signs of a great Council shew forth how for all things which human ingenuity discovers, God calls upon His hidden knowledge, as likewise the Book of Nature, though it stands open truly for all eyes, can be read or understood by only a very few.

As in the human head there are two organs of hearing, two of sight, and two of smell, but onely one of speech, and it were but vain to expect speech from the ears, or hearing from the eyes, so there have been ages which have seen, others which have heard, others again that have smelt and tasted. Now, there remains that in a short and swiftly approaching time honour should be likewise given to the tongue, that what formerly saw, heard, and smelt shall finally speak, after the world shall have slept away the intoxication of her poisoned and stupefying chalice, and with an open heart, bare head, and naked feet shall merrily and joyfully go forth to meet the sun rising in the morning.

CHAPTER IX.

These characters and letters, as God hath here and there incorporated them in the Sacred Scriptures, so hath He imprinted them most manifestly on the wonderful work of creation, on the heavens, the earth, and on all beasts, so that as the mathematician predicts eclipses, so we prognosticate the obscurations of the church, and how long they shall last. From these letters we have borrowed our magick writing, and thence have made for ourselves a new language, in which the nature of things is expressed, so that it is no wonder that we are not so eloquent in other tongues, least of all in this Latin, which we know to be by no means in agreement with that of Adam and of Enoch, but to have been contaminated by the confusion of Babel.[1]

CHAPTER X.

But this also must by no means be omitted, that, while there are yet some eagle's feathers in our way, the which do hinder our purpose, we do exhort to the sole, onely, assiduous, and continual study of the Sacred Scriptures, for he that taketh all his pleasures therein shall know that he hath prepared for himself an excellent way to come into our Fraternity, for this is the whole sum of our Laws, that as there is not a character in that great miracle of the world which has not a claim on the memory, so those are nearest and likest unto us who do make the Bible the rule of their life, the end of all their studies, and the compendium of the universal world, from whom we require not that it should be continually in their mouth, but that they should appropriately apply its true interpretation to all ages of the world, for it is not our custom so to debase the divine oracle, that while there are innumerable expounders of the same, some adhere to the opinions of their party, some make sport of Scripture as if it were a tablet of wax to be indifferently made use of by theologians, philosophers, doctors, and mathematicians. Be it ours rather to bear witness, that from the beginning of the world there hath not been given to man a more excellent, admirable, and wholesome book then the Holy Bible; Blessed is he who possesses it, more blessed is he who reads it, most blessed of all is he who truly understandeth it, while he is most like to God who both understands and obeys it.

CHAPTER XI.

Now, whatsoever hath been said in the Fama, through hatred of impostors, against the transmutation of metals and the supreme medicine of the world, we desire to be so understood, that this so great gift of God we do in no manner set at naught, but as it bringeth not always with it the knowledge of Nature, while this knowledge bringeth forth both that and an infinite number of other natural miracles, it is right that we be rather earnest to attain to the knowledge of philosophy, nor tempt excellent wits to the tincture of metals sooner then to the observation of Nature. He must needs be insatiable to whom neither poverty, diseases, nor danger can any longer reach, who, as one raised above all men, hath rule over that which loth anguish, afflict, and pain others, yet will give himself again to idle things, will build, make wars, and domineer, because he hath of gold sufficient, and of silver an inexhaustible fountain. God judgeth far otherwise, who exalteth the lowly, and casteth the proud into obscurity; to the silent he sendeth his angels to hold speech with them, but the babblers he driveth into the wilderness, which is the judgment due to the Roman impostor who now poureth his blasphemies with open mouth against Christ, nor yet in the full light, by which Germany hath detected his caves and subterranean passages, will abstain from lying, that thereby he may fulfil the measure of his sin, and be found worthy of the axe. Therefore, one day it will come to pass, that the mouth of this viper shall be stopped, and his triple crown shall be brought to nought, of which things more fully when we shall have met together.

CHAPTER XII.

For conclusion of our Confession we must earnestly admonish you, that you cast away, if not all, yet most of the worthless books of pseudo chymists, to whom it is a jest to apply the Most Holy Trinity to vain things, or to deceive men with monstrous symbols and enigmas, or to profit by the curiosity of the credulous; our age doth produce many such, one of the greatest being a stage-player, a man with sufficient ingenuity for imposition; such doth the enemy of human welfare mingle among the good seed, thereby to make the truth more difficult to be believed, which in herself is simple and naked, while falshood is proud, haughty, and coloured with a lustre of seeming godly and humane wisdom. Ye that are wise eschew such books, and have recourse to us, who seek not your moneys, but offer unto you most willingly our great treasures. We hunt not after your goods with invented lying tinctures, but desire to make you partakers of our goods. We do not reject parables, but invite you to the clear and simple explanation of all secrets; we seek not to be received of you, but call you unto our more then kingly houses and palaces, by no motion of our own, but (lest you be ignorant of it) as forced thereto by the Spirit of God, commanded by the testament of our most excellent Father, and impelled by the occasion of this present time.

CHAPTER XIII.

What think you, therefore, O Mortals, seeing that we sincerely confess Christ, execrate the pope, addict ourselves to the true philosophy, lead a worthy life, and dayly call, intreat, and invite many more unto our Fraternity, unto whom the same Light of God likewise appeareth? Consider you not that, having pondered the gifts which are in you, having measured your understanding in the Word of God, and having weighed the imperfection and inconsistencies of all the arts, you may at length in the future deliberate with us upon their remedy, co-operate in the work of God, and be serviceable to the constitution of your time? On which work these profits will follow, that all those goods which Nature hath dispersed in every part of the earth shall at one time and altogether be given to you, *tanquam in centro solis et lunæ*. Then shall you be able to expel from the world all those things which darken human knowledge and hinder action, such as the vain (astronomical) epicycles and eccentric circles.

CHAPTER XIV.

You, however, for whom it is enough to be serviceable out of curiosity to any ordinance, or who are dazzled by the glistering of gold, or who, though now upright, might be led away by such unexpected great riches into an effeminate, idle, luxurious, and pompous life, do not disturb our sacred silence by your clamour, but think, that although there be a medicine which might fully cure all diseases, yet those whom God wishes to try or to chastise shall not be abetted by such an opportunity, so that if we were able to enrich and instruct the whole world, and liberate it from innumerable hardships, yet shall we never be manifested unto any man unless God should favour it, yea, it shall be so far from him who thinks to be partaker of our riches against the will of God that he shall sooner lose his life in seeking us, then attain happiness by finding us.

FRATERNITAS R. C.

Footnotes

1 The original reads *Babylonis confusione*, "by the confusion of Babylon."

Chymische Hoch-
zeit:
Christiani Rosencreütz.
ANNO 1459.

Arcana publicata vilescunt; & gratiam prophanata amittunt.

Ergo: ne Margaritas obijce porcis, seu Asino substerne rosas.

Straßburg/
In Verlägung / Lazari Zetzners.

Anno M. DC. XVI.

THE CHYMICAL MARRIAGE OF CHRISTIAN ROSENCREUTZ.

The whole Rosicrucian controversy centres in this publication, which Buhle describes as "a comic romance of extraordinary talent." It was first published at Strasbourg in the year 1616, but, as will be seen in the seventh chapter, it is supposed to have existed in manuscript as early as 1601-2, thus antedating by a long period the other Rosicrucian books. Two editions of the German original are preserved in the Library of the British Museum, both bearing the date 1616.[1] It was translated into English for the first time in 1690, under the title of

"The Hermetic Romance: or The Chymical Wedding. Written in High Dutch by Christian Rosencreutz. Translated by E. Foxcroft, late Fellow of King's Colledge in Cambridge. Licensed and entered according to Order. Printed by A. Sowie, at the Crooked Billet in Holloway-Lane, Shoreditch; and Sold at the Three-Keys in Nags-Head-Court, Grace-church-street."

It is this translation in substance, that is, compressed by the omission of all irrelevant matter and dispensable prolixities, which I now offer to the reader.

Footnotes
1. "Chymische Hochzeit: Christiani Rosencreutz. Anno 1459. Erstlick Gedrucktzor Strasbourg. Anno M.DC.XVI." The second edition was printed by Conrad Echer.

THE CHYMICAL MARRIAGE OF CHRISTIAN ROSENCREUTZ. ANNO 1459.

Arcana publicata vilescunt, et gratiam prophanata amittunt.
Ergo: ne Margaritas objice porcis, seu Asino substernere rosas.

THE FIRST DAY

Meditatio.

On an evening before Easter-day, I sate at a table, and having in my humble prayer conversed with my Creator and considered many great mysteries (whereof the Father of Lights had shewn me not a few), and being now ready to prepare in my heart, together with my dear Paschal Lamb, a small, unleavened, undefiled cake, all on a sudden ariseth so horrible a tempest, that I imagined no other but that, through its mighty force, the bill whereon my little house was founded would fly all in pieces. But inasmuch as this, and the like, from the devil (who had done me many a spight) was no new thing to me, I took courage, and persisted in my meditation till somebody touched me on the back, whereupon I was so hugely terrified that I durst hardly look about me, yet I shewed myself as cheerful as humane frailty would permit. Now the same thing still twitching me several times by the coat, I glanced back and behold

Praeconissa

it was fair and glorious lady, whose garments were all skye-colour, and curiously bespangled with golden stars. In her right hand she bare a trumpet of beaten gold, whereon a Name was ingraven which I could well read but am forbidden as yet to reveal. In her left hand she had a great bundle of letters in all languages, which she (as I afterwards understood) was to carry into all countries. She had also large and beautiful wings, full of eyes throughout, wherewith she could mount aloft, and flye swifter than any eagle. As soon as I turned about, she looked through her letters, and at length drew out a small one, which, with great reverence, she laid upon the table, and, without one word, departed from me. But in her mounting upward, she gave so mighty a blast on her gallant trumpet that the whole hill echoed thereof, and for a full quarter of an hour afterward I could hardly hear my own words.

In so unlooked for an adventure I was at a loss how to advise myself, and, therefore, fell upon my knees, and besought my Creator to permit nothing contrary to my eternal happiness to befall

Epistola.

me, whereupon, with fear and trembling, I went to the letter, which was now so heavy as almost to outweigh gold. As I was diligently viewing it, I found a little Seal, whereupon was ingraven a curious Cross, with this inscription IN HOC SIGNO ♈ VINCES.

As soon as I espied this sign I was comforted, not being ignorant that it was little acceptable, and much less useful, to the devil. Whereupon I tenderly opened the letter, and within it, in an azure field, in golden letters, found the following verses written:–

> *This day, this day, this, this*
> *The Royal Wedding is.*
> *Art thou thereto by birth inclined,*
> *And unto joy of God design'd?*
> *Then may'st thou to the mountain tend*
> *Whereon three stately Temples stand,*
> *And there see all from end to end.*
> *Keep watch and ward,*
> *Thyself regard;*
> *Unless with diligence thou bathe,*
> *The Wedding can't thee harmless save:*
> *He'll damage have that here delays;*
> *Let him beware too light that weighs.*

Underneath stood *Sponsus* and *Sponsa*.

As soon as I read this letter, I was like to have fainted away, all my hair stood on end, and cold sweat trickled down my whole body. For although I well perceived that this was the appointed wedding whereof seven years before I was acquainted in a bodily vision, and which I had with great earnestness attended, and which, lastly, by the account and calculation of the plannets, I found so to be, yet could I never fore-see that it must happen

under so grievous and perilous conditions. For whereas I before imagined that to be a well-come guest, I needed onely to appear at the wedding, I was now directed to Divine Providence, of which until this time I was never certain. I also found, the more I examined myself, that in my head there was onely gross

misunderstanding, and blindness in mysterious things, so that I was not able to comprehend even those things which lay under my feet, and which I daily conversed with, much less that I should be born to the searching out and understanding of the secrets of

Nature, since, in my opinion, Nature might everywhere find a more vertuous disciple, to whom to intrust her precious, though temporary and changeable treasures. I found also that my bodily behaviour, outward conversation, and brotherly love toward my neighbour was not duly purged and cleansed. Moreover, the tickling of the flesh manifested itself, whose affection was bent only to pomp, bravery, and worldly pride, not to the good of mankind; and I was always contriving how by this art I might in a short time abundantly increase my advantage, rear stately palaces, make myself an everlasting name, and other the like carnal designs. But the obscure words concerning the three Temples did particularly afflict me, which I was not able to make out by any after-speculation. Thus sticking between hope and fear, examining myself again and again, and finding only my own frailty and impotency, and exceedingly amazed at the fore-mentioned threatening, at length I betook myself to my usual course. After I had finished my most fervent prayer, I laid me down in my bed, that so perchance my good angel by the Divine permission might appear, and (as it had formerly happened) instruct me in this affair, which, to the praise of God, did now likewise fall out. For I was yet scarce asleep when me-thought I, together with a numberless multitude of men, lay fettered with great chains in a dark dungeon, wherein we swarmed like bees one over another, and thus rendered each other's affliction more grievous. But although neither I, nor any of the rest, could see one jot, yet I continually heard one heaving himself above the other, when his chains or fetters were become ever so little lighter. Now as I with the rest had continued a good while in this affliction, and each was still reproaching the other with his blindness and captivity, at length we heard many trumpets sounding together, and kettle-drums beating so artificially thereto, that it rejoyced us even in our calamity.

During this noise the cover of the dungeon was lifted up, and a little light let down unto us. Then first might truly have been discerned the bustle we kept, for all went pesle-mesle, and he who perchance had too much heaved up himself was forced down. again under the others' feet. In brief, each one strove to be uppermost, neither did I linger, but, with my weighty fetters, slipt from under the rest, and then heaved myself upon a Stone; howbeit, I was several times caught at by others, from whom, as well as I might, I guarded myself with hands and feet. We imagined that we should all be set at liberty, which yet fell out quite otherwise, for after the nobles who looked upon us through

Mundana affectio.

Preces.

Turris Cœcitas.

Visio per somnium

Illustratio

the hole had recreated themselves with our struggling, a certain hoary-headed man called to us to be quiet, and, having obtained it, began thus to say on:

Magister carceris

> *If wretched mortals would forbear*
> *Themselves to so uphold,*
> *Then sure on them much good confer*
> *My righteous Mother would:*
> *But since the same will not insue,*
> *They must in care and sorrow rue,*
> *And still in prison lie.*
> *Howbeit, my dear Mother will*
> *Their follies over-see,*
> *Her choicest goods permitting still*
> *Too much in Light to be.*
> *Wherefore, in honour of the feast*
> *We this day solemnize,*
> *That so her grace may be increast,*
> *A good deed she'll devise;*
> *For now a cord shall be let down,*
> *And whosoe'er can hang thereon*
> *Shall freely be releast.*

Vide S. Bernard, Serm. 3, de 7 Fragmentis

He had scarce done speaking when an Antient Matron commanded her servants to let down the cord seven times into the dungeon, and draw up whomsoever could hang upon it. Good God! that I could sufficiently describe the hurry that arose amongst us; every one strove to reach the cord, and only hindred each other. After seven minutes a little bell rang, whereupon at the first pull the servants drew up four. At that time I could not come near the cord, having to my huge misfortune betaken myself to the stone at the wall, whereas the cord descended in the middle. The cord was let down the second time, but divers, because their chains were too heavy, and their hands too tender, could not keep hold on it, and brought down others who else might have held on fast enough. Nay, many were forcibly pulled off by those who could not themselves get at it, so envious were we even in this misery. But they of all most moved my compassion whose weight was so heavy that they tore their hands from their bodies and yet could not get up. Thus it came to pass that at these five times very few were drawn up, for, as soon as the sign was given, the

Prima vectura.

Seconda.

servants were so nimble at the draught that the most part tumbled one upon another. Whereupon, the greatest part, and even myself, despaired of redemption, and called upon God to have pitty on us, and deliver us out of this obscurity, who also heard some of us, for when the cord came down the sixth time, some hung themselves fast upon it, and whilst it swung from one side to the other, it came to me, which I suddenly catching, got uppermost, and so beyond all hope came out; whereat I exceedingly rejoyced, perceiving not the wound which in the drawing up I received on my head by a sharp stone, till I, with the rest of the released (as was always before done) was fain to help at the seventh and last pull, at which, through straining, the blood ran down my cloathes. This, nevertheless, through joy I regarded not.

Sexta.

Septima.

Vulnus exturro cæcitatis.

When the last draught, whereon the most of all hung, was finished, the Matron caused the cord to be laid away, and willed her aged son to declare her resolution to the rest of the prisoners, who thus spoke unto them.

Magistræ filius.

> *Ye children dear*
> *All present here,*
> *What is but now compleat and done*
> *Was long before resolved on;*
> *Whate'er my mother of great grace*
> *To each on both sides here hath shown;*
> *May never discontent misplace!*
> *The joyful time is drawing on*
> *When every one shall equal be–*
> *None wealthy, none in penury.*
> *Whoe'er received great commands*
> *Hath work enough to fill his hands*
> *Whoe'er with much hath trusted been,*
> *'Tis well if he may save his skin;*
> *Wherefore, your lamentations cease,*
> *What is't to waite for some few dayes?*

The cover was now again put to and locked, the trumpets and kettle-drums began afresh, yet the bitter lamentation of the prisoners was heard above all, and soon caused my eyes to run over. Presently the Antient Matron, together with her son, sate down, and commanded the Redeemed should be told. As soon as she had written down their number in a gold-yellow tablet, she

Magistra recens et evectos.

Secretarus

Cur non omnes evecti.

demanded everyone's name; this was also written down by a little page. Having viewed us all, she sighed, and said to her son– "Ah, how hardly am I grieved for the poor men in the dungeon! I would to God I durst release them all." Whereunto her son replied – "Mother, it is thus ordained by God, against Whom we may not contend. In case we all of us were lords, and were seated at table, who would there be to bring up the service!" At this his mother held her peace, but soon after she said – "Well, let these be freed from their fetters," which was presently done, and I, though among the last, could not refrain, but bowed myself before the Antient Matron, thanking God that through her had graciously vouchsafed to bring me out of darkness into light. The rest did likewise to the satisfaction of the matron. Lastly, to every one was given a piece of gold for a remembrance, and to spend by the way. On the one side thereof was stamped the rising sun; on the other these three letters D L S; therewith all had license to depart to his own business, with this intimation, that we to the glory of God should benefit our neighbours, and reserve in silence what we had been intrusted with, which we promised to do, and departed one from another. Because of the wounds the fetters had caused me, I could not well go forward, which the matron presently espying, calling me again to her side, said to me – "My son, let not this defect afflict thee, but call to mind thy infirmities, and thank God who hath permitted thee, even in this world, to come into so high a light. Keep these wounds for my sake."

Gratitudo auctoris evecti.

Nummus aureus.

⊙

Deus Lux solis, vel Deo laus semper.

Mandatum Taciturnitatis.

Discessus autoris

Vulnus ex compedibus.

Whereupon the trumpets began again to sound, which so affrighted me that I awoke, and perceived that it was onely a dream, which yet was so impressed on my imagination that I was perpetually troubled about it, and methought I was still sensible of the wounds on my feet. By all these things I well understood that God had vouchsafed me to be present at this mysterious and hidden Wedding, wherefore with childlike confidence I returned thanks to His Divine Majesty, and besought Him that He would preserve me in His fear, daily fill my heart with wisdom and understanding, and graciously conduct me to the desired end. Thereupon I prepared myself for the way, put on my white linnen coat, girded my loyns, with a blood-red ribbon bound cross-ways over my shoulder. In my hat I stuck four red roses, that I might the sooner by this token be taken notice of amongst the throng.

Experget actio.

Solatium.

Precatio.

Præparatio ad iter.

For food I took bread, salt, and water, which by the counsel of an understanding person I had at certain times used, not without profit, in the like occurrences. Before I parted from my cottage, I first, in this my wedding garment, fell down upon my knees, and besought God to vouchsafe me a good issue. I made a vow that if anything should by His Grace be revealed to me, I would imploy it neither to my own honour nor authority in the world, but to the spreading of His name, and the service of my neighbour. With this vow I departed out of my cell with joy.

THE SECOND DAY

Tripudium
Creaturarum
ob nuptias.

In campam.

3 Templa.

I was hardly got out of my cell into a forrest when methought the whole heaven and all the elements had trimmed themselves against this wedding. Even the birds chanted more pleasantly then before, and the young fawns skipped so merrily that they rejoiced my old heart, and moved me also to sing with such a loud voice throughout the whole forrest, that it resounded from all parts, the hills repeating my last words, until at length I espyed a curious green heath, whither I betook myself out of the forrest. Upon this heath stood three tall cedars, which afforded an excellent shade, whereat I greatly rejoyced, for, although I had not gone far, my earnest longing made me faint. As soon as I came somewhat nigh, I espyed a tablet fastened to one of them, on which the following words were written in curious letters:–

Per Sylvam

3 Cedri.

Tabella
mercurialis.

☿

God save thee, Stranger! If thou hast heard anything concerning the nuptials of the King, consider these words. By us doth the Bridegroom offer thee a choice between foure ways, all of which, if thou dost not sink down in the way, can bring thee to his royal court. The first is short but dangerous, and one which will lead thee into rocky places, through which it will be scarcely possible to pass. The second is longer, and takes thee circuitously; it is plain and easy, if by the help of the Magnet, thou turnest neither to left nor right. The third is that truly royal way which through various pleasures and pageants of our King, affords thee a joyful journey; but this so far has scarcely been allotted to one in a thousand. By the fourth shall no man reach

1.

2.

3.

4.

the place, because it is a consuming way, practicable onely for incorruptible bodys. Choose now which thou wilt of the three, and persevere constantly therein, for know whichsoever thou shalt enter, that is the one destined for thee by immutable Fate, nor canst thou go back therein save at great peril to life. These are the things which we would have thee know, but, ho, beware! thou knowest not with how much danger thou dost commit thyself to this way, for if thou knowest thyself by the smallest fault to be obnoxious to the laws of our King, I beseech thee, while it is still possible, to return swiftly to thy house by the way which thou earnest.

As soon as I had read this writing all my joy vanished, and I, who before sang merrily, began inwardly to lament. For although I saw all three ways before me, and it was vouchsafed me to make choice of one, yet it troubled me that in case I went the stony and rocky way, I might get a deadly fall; or, taking the long one, I might wander through bye-ways and be detained in the great journey. Neither durst I hope that I, amongst thousands, should be the one who should choose the Royal way. I saw likewise the fourth before me, but so invironed with fire and exhalation that I durst not draw near it, and, therefore, again and again considered whether I should turn back or take one of the ways before me. I well weighed my own unworthiness, and though the dream, that I was delivered out of the tower, still comforted me, yet I durst not confidently rely upon it. I was so perplexed that, for great weariness, hunger and thirst seized me, whereupon I drew out my bread, cut a slice of it, which a snow-white dove, of whom I was not aware, sitting upon the tree, espyed and therewith came down, betaking herself very familiarly to me, to whom I willingly imparted my food, which she received, and with her prettiness did again a little refresh me. But as soon as her enemy, a most black Raven, perceived it, he straight darted down upon the dove, and taking no notice of me, would needs force away her meat, who could not otherwise guard herself but by flight. Whereupon, both together flew toward the South, at which I was so hugely incensed and grieved, that without thinking, I made haste after the filthy Raven, and so, against my will, ran into one of the fore-mentioned ways a whole field's length. The Raven being thus chased away, and the Dove delivered, I first observed what I had inconsiderately done, and that I was in already

Via authoris eligenda.

Dubium.

Confirmatio

Columba alba arbori mercuriali insidens.

Corvus niger

Versus Meridiem.

54

entered into a way, from which, under peril of punishment, I durst *Autor in* not retire, and though I had still wherewith to comfort myself, *cidit* yet that which was worst of all was, that I had left my bag and bread at the Tree, and could never retrieve them, for as soon as I turned myself about, a contrary wind was so strong against me *2 viam* that it was ready to fell me, but if I went forward, I perceived *incogitanter* no hindrance, wherefore I patiently took up my cross, got upon my feet, and resolved I would use my utmost endeavour to get to my journey's end before night. Now, although many apparent *Compassus.* byways showed themselves, I still proceeded with my compass, and would not budge one step from the meridian line. Howbeit, the way was oftentimes so rugged that I was in no little doubt of it. I constantly thought upon the Dove and Raven, and yet could not search out the meaning, until upon a high hill afar off I espyed *Diversorium* *Occasus.* a stately Portal, to which, not regarding that it was distant from the way I was in, I hasted, because the sun had already hid himself under the hills, and I could elsewhere see no abiding place, which I verily ascribe only to God, Who might have permitted me to go forward, and withheld my eyes that so I might have gazed beside this gate, to which I now made mighty haste, and reached it by so much daylight as to take a competent view of it. It was an exceeding Royal, beautiful Portal, whereon were carved a multitude of most noble figures and devices, every one of which (as I afterwards learned) had its peculiar signification. Above was *Tabula* fixed a pretty large Tablet, with these words, "*Procul hinc procul* *inscriptionis.* *ite profani,*" and more that I was forbidden to relate. As soon as I was come unto the portal, there streight stepped forth one in a *Portitor.* sky-coloured habit, whom I saluted in friendly manner. Though he thankfully returned my greeting, he instantly demanded my *Literæ* Letter of Invitation. O how glad was I that I had brought it with *convocationis.* me! How easily might I have forgotten it as chanced to others, as he himself told me. I quickly presented it, wherewith he was not only satisfied, but showed me abundance of respect, saying, "Come in, my Brother, an acceptable guest you are to me," withal entreating me not to withhold my name from him.

Having replied that I was a Brother of the RED ROSIE CROSS, *Nomen* he both wondred and seemed to rejoyce at it, and then proceeded *authoris.* thus:– "My brother, have you nothing about you wherewith to purchase a token?" I answered my ability was small, but if he saw anything about me he had a mind to, it was at his service. Having

Emitur aqua
Tessera.

Diploma.

Virgo
lucifera.

Porta
secunda.
Tabella.

2 Portitor.

Studio
merentis
Sal humor
Sponso
mittendus
Sal mineralis
Sal
menstrualis.

Porta
clauditur.

requested of me my bottle of water, and I granting it, he gave me a golden token, whereon stood these letters, S.C., entreating me that when it stood me in good stead, I would remember him. After which I asked him how many were got in before me, which he also told me; and lastly, out of meer friendship, gave me a sealed letter to the second Porter. Having lingered some time with him, the night grew on, whereupon a great beacon upon the gate was immediately fired, that if any were still upon the way, he might make haste thither. The road where it finished at the castle was enclosed with walls, and planted with all sorts of excellent fruit trees. On every third tree on each side lanterns were hung up, wherein all the candles were lighted with a glorious torch by a beautiful Virgin, habited in skye-colour, which was so noble and majestic a spectacle that I delayed longer then was requisite. At length, after an advantageous instruction, I departed from the first porter, and so went on the way, until I came to the second gate, which was adorned with images and mystick significations. In the affixed Tablet stood – *Date et dabitur volis.* Under this gate lay a terrible Lyon, chained, who, as soon as he espied me, arose and made at me with great roaring, whereupon the second porter, who lay upon a stone of marble, awaked, and wishing me not to be troubled nor affrighted, drove back the lyon, and having received the letter, which I reached him with trembling hand, he read it, and with great respect spake thus to me:– "Now well-come in God's name unto me the man whom of long time I would gladly have seen!" Meanwhile, he also drew out a token, and asked me whether I could purchase it. But I, having nothing else left but my salt, presented it to him, which he thankfully accepted.

Upon this token again stood two letters, namely, S.M. Being just about to discourse with him, it began to ring in the castle, whereupon the porter counselled me to run apace, or all the paines I had taken would serve to no purpose, for the lights above began already to be extinguished, whereupon I dispatched with much haste that I heeded not the porter; the virgin, after whom all the lights were put out, was at my heels, and I should never have found the way, had not she with her torch afforded me some light. I was more-over constrained to enter the very next to her, and the gates were so suddenly clapt to that a part of my coate was locked out, which I was forced to leave behind me, for neither

Sanctitati
constantia
sponsus
charus.
Spes
charitas.

Castillum

The Lady
Chamberlain

Custos Leo.

Tessera
empta sale.

I nor they who stood ready without and called at the gate could prevail with the porter to open it again. He delivered the keys to the virgin, who took them with her into the court. I again surveyed the gate, which now appeared so rich that the world could not equal it. Just by the door were two columns, on one of which stood a pleasant figure with this inscription, *Congratulor*. On the other side was a statue with countenance veiled, and beneath was written, *Condoleo*. In brief, the inscriptions and figures thereon were so dark and mysterious that the most dexterous man could not have expounded them, yet all these I shall e'er long publish and explain. Under this gate I was again to give my name, which was written down in a little vellum-book, and immediately with the rest dispatched to the Lord Bridegroom. Here I first received the true guest-token, which was somewhat less than the former, but much heavier; upon this stood the letters S. P. N. Besides this, a new pair of shoes were given me, for the floor of the castle was pure shining marble. My old ones I was to give to one of the poor who sate in throngs under the gate. I bestowed them on an old man, after which two pages with as many torches conducted me into a little room, where they willed me to sit down upon a form, and, sticking their torches in two holes made in the pavement, they departed, and left me sitting alone. Soon after I heard a noise but saw nothing; it proved to be certain men who stumbled in upon me, but since I could see nothing I was fain to suffer and attend what they would do with me. Presently finding that they were barbers I intreated them not to jostle me, for I was content to do what they desired, whereupon one of them, whom I yet could not see, gently cut away the hair from the crown of my head, but on my forehead, ears, and eyes he permitted my ice-grey locks to hang. In this first encounter I was ready to despair, for, inasmuch as some of them shoved me so forceably, and were still invisible, I could onely think that God for my curiosity had suffered me to miscarry. The unseen barbers carefully gathered up the hair which was cut off, and carried it away. Then the two pages re-entered and heartily laughed at me for being so terrified. They had scarce spoken a few words with me when again a little bell began to ring, which (as the pages informed me) was to give notice for assembling, whereupon they willed me to rise, and through many walks, doors, and winding stairs lighted me into a spacious hall, where there was a great multitude of guests – emperors, kings,

Promissum authoris.

Comes puer.

Balneatores

Pueri bini.

Pyramides portæ.

Salus per naturam sponsi præ sentandus nuptiis.

Capillus detonsus asservatus.

Triclinium

princes, and lords, noble and ignoble, rich and poor, and all sorts of people, at which I hugely marvelled, and thought to myself, "Ah! how gross a fool hast thou been to ingage upon this journey with so much bitterness and toil, when here are fellows whom thou well knowest, and yet hadst never any reason to esteem, while thou, with all thy prayers and supplications, art hardly got in at last."

This and more the devil at that time injected. Meantime one or other of my acquaintance spake to me:– "Oh! Brother Rosencreutz, art thou here too?" "Yea, my brethren," I replied, "The grace of God hath helped me in also," at which they raised a mighty laughter, looking upon it as ridiculous that there should be need of God in so slight an occasion. Having demanded each of *Impictas* them concerning his way, and finding most of them were forced to *hostum non* clamber over the rocks, certain invisible trumpets began to sound *recta via* to the table, whereupon all seated themselves, every one as he *ingressorum.* judged himself above the rest, so that for me and some other sorry fellows there was hardly a little nook left at the lowermost table. Presently the two pages entred, and one of them said grace in so handsom and excellent a manner as rejoyced the very heart *Quidam* in my body. Howbeit, some made but little reckoning of them, *preces* but fleired and winked one at another, biting their lips within *negligunt.* their hats, and using like unseemly gestures. After this, meat was brought in, and, albeit none could be seen, everything was so orderly managed that it seemed as if every guest had his proper *Ministri* attendant. Now my Artists having somewhat recruited themselves, *invisibles.* *Inebriatorum* and the wine having a little removed shame from their hearts, *gloriatio* they presently began to vaunt of their abilities. One would prove *vana* this, another that, and commonly the most sorry idiots made the loudest noise. When I call to mind what preternatural and impossible enterprises I then heard, I am still ready to vomit at it. In fine, they never kept in their order, but whenever possible a rascal would insinuate himself among the nobles. Every man had his own prate, and yet the great lords were so simple that they believed their pretences, and the rogues became so audacious, that although some of them were rapped over the fingers with a knife, yet they flinched not at it, but when any one perchance had filched a gold-chain, then would all hazard for the like. I saw one who heard the movements of the Heavens, the second could see Plato's Ideas, a third could number the atoms of Democritus.

There were not a few pretenders to perpetual motion. Many an one (in my opinion) had good understanding, but assumed too much to himself to his own destruction. Lastly, there was one who would needs persuade us that he saw the servitors who attended, and would have pursued his contention, had not one of those invisible waiters reached him so handsom a cuff upon his lying muzzle, that not only he, but many who were by him, became mute as mice. It best of all pleased me that those of whom I had any esteem were very quiet in their business, acknowledging themselves to be misunderstanding men for whom the mysteries of nature were too high. In this tumult I had almost cursed the day wherein I came hither, for I could not but with anguish behold that those lewd people were above at the board, but I in my sorry place could not even rest in quiet, one of these rascals scornfully reproaching me for a motley fool. I dreamed not that there was one gate behind through which we must pass, but imagined during the whole wedding I was to continue in this scorn and indignity which I had at no time deserved, either of the Lord Bride-groom or the Bride. And, therefore, I opined he would have done well to seek some other fool than me for his wedding. To such impatience doth the iniquity of this world reduce simple hearts. But this was really one part of the lameness whereof I had dreamed.

Ministri invisibles.

Modestia proborum hospitum.

Impatientia ex iniquitate hominum.

The longer all this clamour lasted, the more it increased. Howbeit, there sate by me a very fine, quiet man, who discoursed of excellent matters, and at length said:– "My Brother, if any one should come now who were willing to instruct these blockish people in the right way, would he be heard?" "No, verily," I replyed. "The world," said he, "is now resolved to be cheated, and will give no ear to those who intend its good. Seest thou that Cock's-comb, with what whimsical figures and foolish conceits he allures others. There one makes mouths at the people with unheard-of mysterious words. Yet the time is now coming when those shameful vizards shall be plucked off, and the world shall know what vagabond imposters were concealed behind them. Then perhaps that will be valued which at present is not esteemed."

Assessor modestus.

Mundus valt decipi.

While he was thus speaking, and the clamour was still increasing, all on a sudden there began in the hall such excellent and stately musick of which, all the days of my life, I never heard the like. Every one held his peace, and attended what would come of it. There were all stringed instruments imaginable, sounding

Musica.

together in such harmony that I forgot myself, and sate so unmovably that those by me were amazed. This lasted nearly half an hour, wherein none of us spake one word, for as soon as anyone was about to open his mouth, he got an unexpected blow.

Mulctæ ab attendentium.

After that space this musick ceased suddenly, and presently before the door of the hall began a great sounding and beating of trumpets, shalms, and kettle-drums, all so master-like as if the Emperor of Rome had been entring. The door opened of itself, and then the noise of the trumpets was so loud that we were hardly able to indure it. Meanwhile, many thousand small tapers came into the hall, marching of themselves in so exact an order as amazed us, till at last the two fore-mentioned pages

Faculæ ad lectum.

Virgo lucifera

with bright torches entred lighting in a most beautiful Virgin, drawn on a gloriously gilded, triumphant self-moving throne. She seemed to me the same who on the way kindled and put out the lights, and that these her attendants were the very ones whom she formerly placed at the trees. She was not now in skye-colour, but in a snow-white, glittering robe, which sparkled of pure gold, and cast such a lustre that we durst not steadily behold it. Both the pages were after the same manner habited, albeit somewhat more slightly. As soon as they were come into the middle of the hall, and were descended from the throne, all the small tapers made obeisance before her, whereupon we all stood up, and she having to us, as we again to her, shewed all respect and reverence, in a most pleasant tone she began thus to speak:–

The Lady Chamberlain

Albedo.

Salutoria hospitum

> *"The King my Lord most gracious,*
> *Who now 's not very far from us,*
> *As also his most lovely Bride,*
> *To him in troth and honour tied,*
> *Already, with great joy indued,*
> *Have your arrival hither view'd;*
> *And do to every one and all*
> *Promise their grace in special;*
> *And from their very heart's desire*
> *You may the same in time acquire,*
> *That so their future nuptial joy*
> *May mixed be with none's annoy."*

Hereupon, with all her small tapers, she again courteously bowed, and presently began thus:–

"In th' Invitation writ you know
That no man called was hereto
Who of God's rarest gifts good store
Had not received long before.
Although we cannot well conceit
That any man's so desperate,
Under conditions so hard,
Here to intrude without regard,
Unless he have been first of all
Prepared for this Nuptial,
And, therefore, in good hopes do dwell
That with all you it will be well;
Yet men are grown so bold and rude,
Not weighing their ineptitude,
As still to thrust themselves in place
Whereto none of them called was.
No cock's-comb here himself may sell,
No rascal in with others steal,
For we resolve without all let
A Wedding pure to celebrate.

So, then, the artists for to weigh,
Scales shall be fixt th' ensuing day;
Whereby each one may lightly find
What he hath left at home behind.
If here be any of that rout,
Who have good cause themselves to doubt,
Let him pack quickly hence aside,
Because in case he longer bide,
Of grace forelorn, and quite undone,
Betimes he must the gantlet run.
If any now his conscience gall,
He shall to-night be left in th' hall,
And be again releast by morn,
Yet so he hither ne'er return.
If any man have confidence,
He with his waiter may go hence,
Who shall him to his chamber light,
Where he may rest in peace to-night."

As soon as she had done speaking, she again made reverence, and sprung chearfully into her throne, after which the trumpets began again to sound, and conducted her invisibly away, but the most part of the small tapers remained, and still one of them accompanied each of us. In our perturbation, 'tis scarcely possible to express what pensive thoughts and gestures were amongst us, yet most part resolved to await the scale, and in case things sorted not well to depart (as they hoped) in peace. I had soon cast up Autor humiliat se. my reckoning, and seeing my conscience convinced me of all ignorance and unworthiness, I purposed to stay with the rest in the hall, and chose rather to content myself with the meal I had taken than to run the risk of a future repulse. After every one by his small taper had been severally conducted to a chamber (each, as I since understood, into a peculiar one), there staid nine of us, including he who discoursed with me at the table. Although our small tapers left us not, yet within an hour's time one of the pages came in, and, bringing a great bundle of cords with him, first demanded whether we had concluded to stay there, which when we had with sighs affirmed, he bound each of us in a several place, and so went away with our tapers, leaving us poor wretches in darkness. Then first began some to perceive the imminent danger, and myself could not refrain tears, for, although we were not forbidden to speak, anguish and affliction suffered none of us to utter one word. The cords were so wonderfully made that none could cut them, much less get them off his feet, yet this comforted me, that the future gain of many an one who had now betaken himself to rest would prove little to his satisfaction, but we by one night's pennance might expiate all our presumption. At length in my sorrowful thoughts I fell asleep, during which I had a dream *Somnium* which I esteem not impertinent to recount. Methought I was upon *typicum.* an high mountain, and saw before me a great valley, wherein were *What will* gathered an unspeakable multitude, each of whom had at his head *be the* a string by which he was hanging. Now one hung high, another *issue of the* low, some stood even quite upon the earth. In the air there flew up *probatory* and down an ancient man, who had in his hand a pair of sheers, *beam? He* wherewith here he cut one's and there another's thread. Now he *that climbs* that was nigh the earth fell without noise, but when this happened *high hath a* to the high ones the earth quaked at their fall. To some it came *great fall.* to pass that their thread was so stretched they came to the earth before it was cut. I took pleasure at this tumbling, and it joyed

62

me at the heart when he who had over-exalted himself in the air, of his wedding, got so shameful a fall that it carried even some of his neighbours along with him. In like manner it rejoyced me that he who had kept so near the earth could come down so gently that even his next men perceived it not. But in my highest fit of jollity, I was unawares jogged by one of my fellow-captives, upon

Experget. which I waked and was much discontented with him. Howbeit, I considered my dream and recounted it to my brother, who lay by me on the other side, and who hoped some comfort might thereby be intended. In such discourse we spent the remaining part of the night, and with longing expected the day.

THE THIRD DAY.

As soon as the lovely day was broken, and the bright sun, having raised himself above the hills, had betaken himself to his appointed office, my good champions began to rise and leisurely make themselves ready unto the inquisition. Whereupon, one after another they came again into the hall, and giving us a good morrow, demanded how we had slept; and having espied our *Colloquium* bonds, some reproved us for being so cowardly, that we had not, *surgentium.* as they, hazarded upon all adventures. Howbeit, some, whose hearts still smote them, made no loud cry of the business. We excused ourselves with our ignorance, hoping we should soon be set at liberty and learn wit by this disgrace, that they also had not altogether escaped, and perhaps their greatest danger was still to be

Cantus. expected. At length all being assembled, the trumpets began again to sound and the kettle-drums to beat, and we imagined that the Bride-groom was ready to present himself, which, nevertheless,

Virgo was a huge mistake, for again it was the Virgin, who had arrayed
lucifera. herself all in red velvet, and girded herself with a white scarfe.
The Lady Upon her head she had a green wreath of laurel, which much
Chamberlain became her. Her train was no more of small tapers, but consisted of two hundred men in harness, all cloathed, like herself, in red and white. As soon as they were alighted from the throne, she comes streight to us prisoners, and, after she had saluted us, said in few words:– "That some of you have been sensible of your *Solatur* wretched condition is pleasing to my most mighty Lord, and he *humiles.*

is also resolved you shall fare the better for it." Having espied me in my habit, she laughed and spake:– "Good lack! Hast thou also submitted thyself to the yoke! I imagined thou wouldst have made thyself very snug," which words caused my eyes to run over. After this she commanded we should be unbound, cuppled together, and placed in a station where we might well behold the scales. "For," said she, "it may fare better with them than with the presumptuous who yet stand at liberty."

Libra aurea.
Meantime the scales, which were intirely of gold, were hung up in the midst of the hall. There was also a little table covered with red velvet, and seven weights thereon – first of all stood *7 Pondera.* a pretty great one, then four little ones, lastly, two great ones severally, and these weights in proportion to their bulk were so heavy that no man can believe or comprehend it. Each of the *Satellites.* harnised men carried a naked sword and a strong rope. They were distributed according to the number of weights into seven bands, and out of every band was one chosen for their proper weight, after which the Virgin again sprung up into her high throne, and *Pendesantur artifices* one of the pages commanded each to place himself according to his order, and successively step into the scale. One of the Emperors, making no scruple, first bowed himself a little towards *1. Cæsar.* the Virgin, and in all his stately attire went up, whereupon each captain laid in his weight, which (to the wonder of all) he stood out. But the last was too heavy for him, so that forth he must, and that with such anguish that the Virgin herself seemed to pitty him, yet was the good Emperor bound and delivered to the sixth band. *2. Cæsar.* Next him came forth another Emperor, who stept hautily into the scale, and, having a thick book under his gown, he imagined not to fail; but, being scarce able to abide the third weight, he was unmercifully slung down, and his book in that affrightment slipping from him, all the soldiers began to laugh, and he was delivered up bound to the third band. Thus it went also with some others of the Emperors, who were all shamefully laughed *3. Alii Cæsares.* at and made captive. After these comes forth a little short man, *4. Cæsar.* with a curled brown beard, an Emperor too, who, after the usual reverence, got up and held out so stedfastly that methought had there been more weights he would have outstood them. To him the Virgin immediately arose and bowed before him, causing him to put on a gown of red velvet, then reaching him a branch of laurel, whereof she had good store upon her throne, on the steps of which

she willed him to sit down. How after him it fared with the rest of the Emperors, Kings, and Lords, would be too long to recount; few of those great personages held out, though sundry eminent vertues were found in many. Everyone who failed was miserably laughed at by the bands. After the inquisition had passed over the gentry, the learned, and unlearned, in each condition one, it may be, two, but mostly none, being found perfect, it came to those *Proba* vagabond cheaters and rascally *Lapidem Spilalanficum* makers, *falsariorum.* who were set upon the scale with such scorn, that for all my grief I was ready to burst my belly with laughing, neither could the prisoners themselves refrain, for the most part could not abide that severe trial, but with whips and scourges were jerked out of the scale. Thus of so pert a throng so few remained that I am ashamed to discover their number. Howbeit, there were persons of quality *Nobiles* also amongst them who, notwithstanding, were also honoured *nihilominu* with velvet robes and wreaths of lawrel. *ornantur.*

The inquisition being finished, and none but we poor coupled hounds standing aside, one of the captains stept forth, and said:– "Gratious madam, if it please your ladyship, let these poor men, *Proba* who acknowledged their misunderstanding, be set upon the scale *Humilium.* also without danger of penalty, and only for recreation's sake, if perchance anything right be found among them." At this I was in great perplexity, for in my anguish this was my only comfort, that I was not to stand in such ignomity, or be lashed out of the scale. Yet since the Virgin consented, so it must be, and we being untied were one after another set up. Now, although the most part miscarried, they were neither laughed at nor scourged, but peaceably placed on one side. My companion was the fifth, who *Socius* held out bravely, whereupon all, but especially the captain who *Autoris.* made the request for us, applauded him, and the Virgin showed him the usual respect. After him two more were despatched in *Autor.* an instant. But I was the eighth, and as soon as (with trembling) I stepped up, my companion, who already sat by in his velvet, looked friendly upon me, and the Virgin herself smiled a little. But, for as much as I outstayed all the weights, the Virgin commanded them to draw me up by force, wherefore three men moreover hung on the other-side of the beam, and yet could nothing prevail. Whereupon one of the pages immediately stood up, and cryed out *That is he.* exceeding loud, "THAT IS HE," upon which the other replyed: "Then let him gain his liberty!" which the Virgin accorded, and being received with due ceremonies, the choice was given me to release one of the captives, whomsoever I pleased, whereupon I made no long deliberations, but elected the first Emperor, whom *Probatissimus.* I had long pittied, who was immediately set free, and with all respect seated among us. Now, the last being set up the weights proved too heavy for him; meanwhile the Virgin espied my roses, which I had taken out of my hat into my hands, and thereupon by her page graciously requested them of me, which I readily sent *Autor rosam* her. And so this first act was finished about ten in the forenoon. *suam donat virgini.*

Liberat, 1. Cæsarem.

Hora, 10. Actus.

The trumpets again began to sound, which, nevertheless, we could not as yet see. Meantime the bands were to step aside with their prisoners and expect the judgment, after which a council of the seven captains and ourselves was set, with the Virgin as president, whereat it was concluded that all the principal lords should with befitting respect be led out of the castle, that others *Judicium de* should be stripped and caused to run out naked, while others yet *reprobatis.* with rods, whips, or dogs, should be hunted out. Those who the day before willingly surrendered themselves might be suffered to depart without any blame, but those presumptuous ones, and they who had behaved themselves so unseemly at dinner, should be punished in body and life according to each man's demerit. This opinion pleased the Virgin well, and obtained the upper hand. There was moreover another dinner vouchsafed them, the execution itself being deferred till noon. Herewith the senate arose, and the Virgin, together with her attendants, returned to her usual quarter. The uppermost table in the room was allotted to us till the business was fully dispatched, when we should be conducted to the Lord Bride-groom and Bride, with which we were well content. The prisoners were again brought into the *Prandium.* hall, and each man seated according to his quality. They were enjoyned to behave somewhat more civilly than they had done the day before, which admonishment they needed not, for they had already put up their pipes, and this I can boldly say, that commonly those who were of highest rank best understood how to comport themselves in so unexpected a misfortune. Their *Ministri* treatment was but indifferent, yet with respect, neither could *invisibles* they see their attendants, who were visible to us, whereat I was *visibles.* exceeding joyful. Although fortune had exalted us, we took not upon us more than the rest, advising them to be of good cheer,

Proborum exaltatio.
and comforting them as well as we could, drinking with them to try if the wine might make them cheerful. Our table was covered with red velvet, beset with drinking cups of pure silver and gold, which the rest could not behold without amazement and anguish. Ere we had seated ourselves in came the two pages, presenting every one, in the Bride-groom's behalf, the Golden Fleece with a flying Lyon, requesting us to wear them at the table, and to observe the reputation and dignity of the order which his Majesty *Remuneratio a sponso.* had vouchsafed us and would ratify with sutable ceremonies. This we received with profoundest submission, promising to perform whatever his Majesty should please. Beside these, the noble page had a schedule wherein we were set down in order. Now because our entertainment was exceeding stately, we demanded one of the pages whether we might have leave to send some choice bit to our friends and acquaintance, who making no difficulty, every one sent by the waiters; howbeit the receivers saw none of them; and forasmuch as they knew not whence it came, I was myself desirous to carry somewhat to one of them, but, as soon as I was *Autori denegatur communicatio erga reprobos.* risen, one of the waiters was at my elbow, desiring me to take friendly warning, for in case one of the pages had seen it, it would have come to the King's ear, who would certainly take it amiss of me; but since none had observed it save himself, he purposed not to betray me, and that I must for the time to come have better regard to the dignity of the order. With these words, the servant did really so astonish me that for long I scarce moved upon my seat, yet I returned him thanks for his faithful warning as well as I was able. Soon after the drums began to beat, wherefore we prepared ourselves to receive the Virgin, who now came in with her train, *Virgo lucifera. The Lady Chamberlain.* upon her high seat, one of the pages bearing before her a very tall goblet of gold, and the other a patent in parchment. Being now after a marvellous artificial manner alighted from her seat, she takes the goblet from the page and presents it in the King's behalf, saying that it was brought from his Majesty, and that in honour of *Calix obambulans.* him we should cause it to go round. Upon the cover of this goblet stood Fortune curiously cast in gold, who had in her hand a red flying ensign, for which cause I drunk somewhat the more sadly, as having been too well acquainted with Fortune's waywardness. But the Virgin who also was adorned with the Golden Fleece and *Ornatus virginis.* Lyon, hereupon began to distinguish the patent which the other *Reprobi dividuntur.* page held into two different parts, out of which thus much was read before the first company:–

That they should confess that they had too lightly given credit
to false, fictitious books, had assumed too much to themselves,

Affectibus   *and so come into this castle uninvited, and perhaps designing*
mundanis   *to make their markets here and afterwards to live in the greater*
pride and lordliness. Thus one had seduced another, and plunged
him into disgrace and ignominy, wherefore they were deservedly
to be soundly punished – all which they, with great humility,
readily acknowledged, and gave their hands upon it, after which
a severe check was given to the rest, much to this purpose:–

That they were convinced in their consciences of forging *Alterius partis.*
false, fictitious books, had befooled and cheated others, thereby
diminishing regal dignity amongst all. They knew what ungodly,
deceitful figures they had made use of; not even sparing the
Divine Trinity. It was also clear as day with what practices they
had endeavoured to ensnare the guests; in like manner, it was
manifest to all the world that they wallowed in open whoredom,
adultery, gluttony, and other uncleannesses. In brief, they had
disparaged Kingly Majesty, even amongst the common sort, and
therefore should confess themselves to be convicted vagabond-
cheats, and rascals, for which they deserved to be cashiered from
the company of civil people, and severely to be punished.

The good Artists were loath to come to this confession, but
inasmuch as the Virgin not only herself threatened, and sware their
death, but the other party also vehemently raged at them, crying
that they had most wickedly seduced them out of the Light, they
at length, to prevent a huge misfortune, confessed the same with
Excusatio.   dolour, yet alledged their actions should not be animadverted
upon in the worst sense, for the Lords were resolved to get into
the castle, and had promised great sums of money to that effect,
each one had used all craft to seize upon something, and so things
were brought to the present pass. Thus they had disserved no more
than the Lords themselves. Their books also sold so mightily that
whoever had no other means to maintain himself was fain to
ingage in this consonage. They hoped, moreover, they should
be found no way to have miscarried, as having behaved towards
the Lords, as became servants, upon their earnest entreaty. But
answer was made that his Royal Majesty had determined to
punish all, albeit one more severely than another. For although *Refutatio.*
what they had alledged was partly true, and therefore the Lords
should not wholly be indulged, yet they had good reason to

prepare themselves for death, who had so presumptuously obtruded themselves, and perhaps seduced the ignorant against their will. Thereupon many began most pitteously to lament and prostrate themselves, all which could avail them nothing, and I much marvelled how the Virgin could be so resolute, when their misery caused our eyes to run over. She presently dispatched her page, who brought with him all the cuirassiers which had been appointed at the scales, who were each commanded to take his own man, and, in an orderly procession, conduct him into her great garden. Leave was given to my yesterday companions to go out into the garden unbound, and be present at the execution of the sentence. When every man was come forth, the Virgin mounted up into her high throne, requesting us to sit down upon the steps, and appear at the judgment. The goblet was committed to the pages' keeping, and we went forth in our robes upon the throne, which of itself moved so gently as if we had passed in the air, till we came into the garden, where we arose altogether. This garden was not extraordinarily curious, only it pleased me that the trees were planted in so good order. Besides there ran in it a most costly fountain, adorned with wonderful figures and inscriptions and strange characters (which, God willing, I shall mention in a future book). In this garden was raised a wooden scaffold, hung with curiously painted figured coverlets. There were four galleries made one over another; the first was more glorious than the rest and covered with a white Taffata curtain, so that we could not perceive who was behind it. The second was empty and uncovered, while the two last were draped with red and blew Taffata. As soon as we were come to the scaffold the Virgin bowed herself down to the ground, at which we were mightily terrified, for we could easily guess that the King and Queen must not be far off. We also having duely performed our reverence, the Virgin led us by the winding stairs into the second gallery, where she placed herself uppermost, and us in our former order. But how the emperor whom I had released behaved towards me, I cannot relate for fear of slander, for he might well imagine in what anguish he now should have been, and that only through me he had attained such dignity and worthiness. Meantime, the virgin who first brought me the invitation, and whom I had hitherto never since seen, stepped in, and giving one blast upon her trumpet declared the sentence with a very loud voice:–

Dolor de sententia.

Spectatores.

Hortus.

Executio sententiarum.

Autor promittit alter librum.

Gratitudo Cæsaris erga liberatorem.

"The King's Majesty, my most gratious Lord, could from his heart wish that all here assembled had, upon his Majestie's invitation, presented themselves so qualified that they might have adorned his nuptial and joyous Feast. But since it hath otherwise pleased Almighty God, he hath not wherewith to murmur, but is forced, contrary to his inclination, to abide by the antient and laudable constitutions of this Kingdom, albeit, that his Majesty's clemency may be celebrated, the usual sentence *Sententia* shall be considerably lenified. He vouchsafes to the Lords and *magnatum.* Potentates not only their lives intirely, but also freely dismisses them, courteously intreating your Lordships not to take it in evil part that you cannot be present at his Feast of Honour. Neither is your reputation hereby prejudiced, although you be rejected by this our Order, since we cannot at once do all things, and forasmuch as your Lordships have been seduced by base rascals, it shall not pass unrevenged. Furthermore, his Majesty resolveth shortly to communicate with you a Catalogue of Hereticks, or *Index Expurgatorius*, that you may with better judgment discern between good and evil. And because his Majesty also purposeth to rummage his library, and offer the seductive writings to Vulcan, he courteously entreats every one of you to put the same in execution with your own, whereby it is to be hoped that all evil and mischief may be remedied. And you are admonished never henceforth so inconsiderately to covet entrance hither, least the former excuse of seducers be taken from you. In fine, as the estates of the Land have still somewhat to demand of your Lordships, his Majesty hopes that no man will think it much to redeem himself with a chain, or what else he hath about him, and so, in friendly manner, depart from us.

"The others who stood not at the first, third, and fourth weight, *Sententia, 2* his Majesty will not so lightly dismiss, but that they also may experience his gentleness, it is his command to strip them naked, and so send them forth. Those who in the second and fifth weight were found too light shall, besides stripping, be noted with one or more brands, according as each was lighter or heavier. They who were drawn up by the sixth or seventh shall be somewhat more *4.* gratiously dealt with, and so forward, for unto every combination there is a certain punishment ordained. They who yesterday separated themselves of their own accord shall go at liberty *6.* without blame. Finally, the convicted vagabond-cheats, who

Oratio ad judicados.

3

5.

could move up none of the weights, shall be punished, in body and life, with sword, halter, water, and rods, and such execution of judgment shall be inviolably observed for an example unto others."

Finis habiti judici.

Herewith one virgin broke her wand; the other, who read the sentence, blew her trumpet, and stepped with profound reverence towards the curtain. Now this judgment being read over, the *Reorum* Lords were well satisfied, for which cause they gave more than *mores.* they were desired, each one redeeming himself with chains,

Ministrorum mores

jewels, gold, monies, and other things, and with reverence they took leave. Although the King's servants were forbidden to jear any at his departure, some unlucky birds could not hold laughing, and certainly it was sufficiently ridiculous to see them pack away with such speed, without once looking behind them. At the door was given to each of them a draught of FORGETFULNESS, *Haustus* that he might have no further memory of misfortune. After these *oblivionis* the volunteers departed, who, because of their ingenuity, were suffered to pass, but so as never to return in the same fashion, albeit if to them (as likewise to the others) anything further were revealed, they should be well-come guests.

Damnati.

Meanwhile, others were stripping, in which also an inequality, according to demerit, was observed. Some were sent away naked, without other hurt; others were driven out with small bells; some again were scourged forth. In brief, the punishments were so various, that I am not able to recount them all. With the last a somewhat longer time was spent, for whilst some were hanging, some beheading, some forced to leap into the water, much time was consumed. Verily, at this execution my eyes ran over, not indeed in regard of the punishment which impudency well deserved, but in contemplation of human blindness, in that we are continually busying ourselves over that which since the first fall

Commiserationis hath been sealed to us. Thus the garden which lately was quite full *expositio* was soon emptied. As soon as this was done, and silence had been kept for the space of five minutes, there came forward a beautiful snow-white Unicorn, with a golden collar, ingraved *Unicorna.* with certain letters, about his neck. He bound himself down upon

Leo.

his fore-feet, as if hereby he had shown honour to the Lyon, who stood so immoveably upon the fountain that I took him to be stone or brass, but who immediately took the naked sword which he bare in his paw, brake it into two in the middle, the two pieces *Machæra.*

whereof sunk into the fountain, after which he so long reared until a white Dove brought a branch of olive in her bill, which the Lyon devoured in an instant, and so was quieted. The Unicorn returned to his place with joy, while our Virgin led us down by the winding staires from the scaffold, and so we again made our reverence towards the curtain. We washed. our hands and heads in the fountain, and thereby waited in order till the King through a secret gallery returned into his hall, and then we also, with choice musick, pomp, state, and pleasant discourse, were conducted into our former lodging. Here, that the time might not seem too long to us, the Virgin bestowed on each of us a noble Page, not only richly habited but also exceeding learned, and able aptly to discourse on all subjects, so that we had reason to be ashamed of ourselves. These were commanded to lead us up and down the castle, yet only in certain places, and, if possible, to shorten the time according to our desire. Meantime, the Virgin took leave, promising to be with us again at supper, and after that to celebrate the ceremonies of hanging up the weights, while on the morrow we should be presented to the King. Each of us now did what best pleased him, one part viewing the excellent paintings, which they copied for themselves, and considered what the wonderful characters might signify, others recruiting themselves with meat and drink. I caused my Page to conduct me, with my Companion, up and down the castle, of which walk it will never repent me so long as I live. Besides many other glorious antiquities, the Royal Sepulcher was shewed me, by which I learned more than is extant in all books. There in the same place stands the glorious Phœnix, of which two years since I published a small discourse, and am resolved, in case this narrative prove useful, to set forth several treatises concerning the Lyon, Eagle, Griffon, Falcon, &c., together with their draughts and inscriptions. It grieves me also for my other consorts that they neglected such pretious treasures. I indeed reaped the most benefit by my Page, for according as each one's genius lay, so he led his intrusted one into the quarters pleasing to him. Now the kyes hereunto belonging were committed to my Page, and, therefore, this good fortune happened to me before the rest, for though he invited others to come in, yet they imagining such tombs to be only in the churchyard, thought they should well enough get thither when ever anything was to be seen there. Neither shall these monuments be with-held from my

Columba.

Discessus ab hoc acta

Discessus virgini luciferæ.

Hospitum modi in delectamentis.

Autoris.

Libellus de Phœnice.

Usus eorum quæ autor vidit.

thankful schollars. The other thing that was shewed us two was the noble Library as it was altogether before the Reformation, of which I have so much the less to say, because the catalogue is shortly to be published. At the entry of this room stands a great Book the like whereof I never saw, in which all the figures, rooms, portals, writings, riddles, and the like, to be seen in the whole castle are delineated. In every book stands its author painted, whereof many were to be burnt, that even their memory might be blotted out from amongst the righteous. Having taken a full view, and being scarce gotten forth, there comes another Page, and having whispered somewhat in our Page's ear, he delivered up the kyes to him, who immediately carried them up the winding stairs; but our Page was very much out of countenance, and we, setting hard upon him with intreaties, he declared to us that the King's Majesty would by no means permit that either the library or sepulchers should be seen by man, and he besought us as we tendered his life to discover it not to anyone, he having already utterly denied it; whereupon both of us stood hovering between joy and fear, yet it continued in silence, and no man made further inquiry about it. Thus in both places we consumed three hours, and now, although it had struck seven, nothing was hitherto given us to eat, but our hunger was abated by constant revivings, and I could be content to fast all my life with such an entertainment. About this time the curious fountains, mines, and all kind of art shops were also shown us, of which there was none but surpassed all our arts even if melted into one mass. Every chamber was built in semi-circle, that so they might have before their eyes the costly clock-work which was erected upon a fair turret in the centre, and regulate themselves according to the course of the planets which were to be seen on it in a glorious manner. At length I came into a spacious room, in the middle whereof stood a terestrial globe, whose diameter contained thirty foot, albeit near half, except a little which was covered with the steps, was let into the earth. Two men might readily turn it about, so that more of it was never to be seen but so much as was above the horizon. I could not understand whereto those ringlets of gold (which were upon it in several places) served, at which my Page laughed, and advised me to view them more narrowly, when I found there my native country noted with gold also, whereupon my companion sought his and found that too. The same happened to others who stood by, and

Fastidium
pulsum
egregiis
spectaculis.

Officinarum
constitutarum
finis.

Globus
terrenus.

73

the Page told us that it was yesterday declared to the King's Majesty by their old astronomer Atlas, that all the gilded points did exactly answer to their native countries, and, therefore, he, as soon as he perceived that I undervalued myself, but that nevertheless there stood a point upon my native country, moved one of the captains to intreat for us to be set upon the scale at all adventures, especially seeing one of our native countries had a notable good mark. And truly it was not without cause that he, the Page of greatest power, was bestowed on me. For this I returned

Excellentia patriæ autoris.

him thanks, and looking more diligently upon my native country, I found that, besides the ringlets, there were also certain delicate streaks upon it. I saw much more even upon this globe than I am willing to discover. Let each man take into consideration why every city produceth not a philosopher. After this he led us within the globe, for on the sea there was a tablet (whereon stood three dedications and the author's name) which a man might gently lift up, and by a little board go into the center, which was capable of four persons, being nothing but a round board whereon we could sit and at ease by broad daylight (it was now already dark)

Quid in glob.

contemplate the stars, which seemed like mere carbuncles glittering in an agreeable order, and moving so gallantly that I had scarce any mind ever to go out again, as the Page afterwards told the Virgin, and with which she often twitted me, for it was already supper time and I was almost the last at table. The waiters treated me with so much reverence and honour that for shame I durst not look up. To speak concerning the musick, or the rest of that magnificent entertainment, I hold needless, because it is not possible sufficiently to express it. In brief there was nothing there but art and amenity. After we had each to other related our employment since noon (howbeit, not a word was spoken of the library and monuments), being already merry with wine, the

Reverentia in convivio exhibita auctoris.

The Lady Chamberlain

Virgin began thus:– "My Lords, I have a great contention with one of my sisters. In our chamber we have an eagle, whom we cherish with such diligence that each of us is desirous to be the best beloved, and upon that score have many a squabble. On a day we concluded to go both together to him, and toward whom he should show himself most friendly, hers should he properly be. This we did, and I, as commonly, bare in my hand a branch of lawrel, but my sister had none. As soon as he espyed us both, he gave my sister another branch which he had in his beak, and

Perplexed speeches, or intricate questions.

offered at mine, which I gave him. Each of us hereupon imagined herself best beloved of him. Which way am I to resolve myself?"

This modest proposal pleased us mightly well, and each one would gladly have heard the solution, but inasmuch as all looked upon me, and desired to have the beginning from me, my mind was so extreamly confounded that I knew not what to do but propound another in its stead, and said, therefore:– "Gracious Lady, your Ladyship's question were easily to be resolved if one thing did not perplex me. I had two companions who both loved me exceedingly; they being doubtful which was most dear to me, concluded to run to me unawares, and that he whom I should then embrace should be the right; this they did, yet one of them could not keep pace with the other, so he staid behind and wept; the other I embraced with amazement. When they had afterwards discovered the business to me, I knew not how to resolve, and have hitherto let it rest in this manner till I may find some good advice herein."

Autoris griphus.

The Author's counter-demand.

The Virgin wondered at it, and well observed where about I was, upon which she replied, that we should both be quit, and then desired the solution from the rest. But I had already made them wise, wherefore the next began thus– "In my city a Virgin was condemned to death, but the judge being pittiful towards her, proclaimed that if any man desired to be her champion, he should have free leave. Now she had two lovers; one made himself ready, and came into the lists to expect his adversary; afterwards the other presented himself, but coming too late, resolved nevertheless to fight, and suffer himself to be vanquished that the Virgin's life might be preserved, which succeeded accordingly. Thereupon each challenged her, and now, my lords, instruct me to which of them of right she belongeth." The Virgin could hold no longer, but said:– "I thought to have gained much information, and am my self gotten into the net; yet I would gladly hear whether there be any more behind." "Yes, that there is," answered the third, "a stranger adventure hath not been recounted then that which happened to myself. In my youth I loved a worthy maid, and that my love might attain its end I made use of an ancient matron, who easily brought me to her. Now it happened that the maid's brethren came in upon us as we three were together, and were in such a rage that they would have taken my life, but, on my vehement supplication, they at length forced me to swear to

Griphus, 3.

Griphus, 4.

take each of them for a year to my wedded wife. Now, tell me, my Lords, should I take the old or the young one first?" We all laughed sufficiently at this riddle, yet none would undertake to unfold it, and the fourth began. "In a certain city there dwelt an *Griphus, 5.* honourable lady, beloved of all, but especially of a noble young man, who would needs be too importunate with her. At length she gave him this determination, that in case he would, in a cold winter, lead her into a fair green garden of Roses, then he should obtain, but if not he must resolve never to see her more. The noble man travelled into all countries to find one who might perform this, till at length he lite upon a little old man who promised to do it for him, in case he would assure him of half his estate, which he having consented to the other was as good as his word. Whereupon he invited the Lady home to his garden, where, contrary to her expectation, she found all things green, pleasant, and warm; and remembring her promise, she only requested that she might once more return to her lord, to whom with sighs and tears she bewailed her lamentable condition. Her lord, sufficiently perceiving her faithfulness, dispatched her back to her lover, who had so dearly purchased her, that she might give him satisfaction, when the husband's integrity so mightily affected the noble man that he thought it a sin to touch so honest a wife, and sent her home with honour to her lord. The little man, perceiving such faith in all these, would not, how poor soever he were, be the least, but restored the noble man all his goods, and went his way. Now, my lords, which of these persons showed the greatest ingenuity?" Here our tongues were quite cut off, neither would the Virgin make any reply but that another should go on; wherefore the fifth *Griphus, 6.* began:– "I desire not to make long work. Who hath the greater joy, he that beholdeth what he loveth, or he that only thinketh on it?" "He that beholdeth it," said the Virgin. "Nay," answered I, and hereupon rose a contest till the sixth called out:– "My lords, I *7.* am to take a wife; I have before me a maid, a married wife, and a widdow; ease me of this doubt, and I will help to order the rest." *8.* "It goes well there," replied the seventh, "when a man hath his choice, but with me the case is otherwise. In my youth I loved a fair and virtuous virgin, and she me in like manner; howbeit, because of her friends' denyal, we could not come together in wedlock, whereupon she was married to another, who maintained her honourably and with affection, till she came into the pains of childbirth, which went so hard with her that all thought she was dead, so with much state and mourning she was interred. Now, I thought with myself, during her life thou couldst have no part in this woman, but dead as she is, thou mayst embrace her sufficiently, whereupon I took my servant with me, who dug her up by night. Having opened the coffin and locked her in my arms, I found some little motion in her heart, which increased from my warmth, till I perceived she was indeed alive. I quietly bore her home, and after I had warmed her chilled body with a costly bath of herbs, I committed her to my mother until she brought forth a fair son, whom I caused faithfully to be nursed. After two days (she being then in a mighty amazement) I discovered to her all the affair, requesting that for the time to come she would live with me as a wife, against which she excepted thus, in case it should be grievous to her husband, who had maintained her well and honourably, but if it could otherwise be, she was the present obliged in love to one as well as the other. After two months (being then to make a journey elsewhere) I invited her husband as a guest, and amongst other things demanded of him whether if his deceased wife should come home again he could be content to receive her, and he affirming it with tears and lamentations, I brought him his wife and son, recounting all the fore-passed business, and intreating him to ratifie with his consent my fore-purposed espousals. After a long dispute he could not beat me from my right, but was fain to leave me the wife. But still the contest was about the son." Here the Virgin interrupted him and said:– "It makes me wonder how you could double the afflicted man's grief." Upon this there arose a dispute amongst us, the most part affirming he had done but right. "Nay," said he, "I freely returned him both his wife and son. Now tell me, my lords, was my honesty or this man's joy the greater?" These words so mightily cheared the Virgin that she caused a health to go round, after which other proposals went on somewhat perplexedly, so that I could not retain them all; yet this comes to my mind, that one told how a few years before he had seen a physitian, who bought a parcel of wood against winter, with which he warmed himself all winter long; but as soon as spring returned he sold the very same wood again, and so had the use of it for nothing. "Here must needs be skill," said the Virgin, "but the time is now past." "Yea," replied my companion, "whoever understands how to

9.

77

resolve all the riddles may give notice of it by a proper messenger; I conceive he will not be denied." At this time they began to say grace, and we arose altogether from the table rather satisfied and merry than glutted; it were to be wished that all invitations and feastings were thus kept. Having taken some few turns up and down the hall, the Virgin asked us whether we desired to begin the wedding. "Yes," said one, "noble and vertuous lady;" whereupon she privately dispatched a Page, and, meantime, proceeded in discourse with us. In brief, she was become so familiar that I adventured and requested her Name. The Virgin smiled at my curiosity, and replyed:– "My name contains five and fifty, and yet hath only eight letters; the third is the third part of the fifth, which added to the sixth will produce a number, whose root shall exceed the third itself by just the first, and it is the half of the fourth. Now the fifth and seventh are equal, the last and first also equal, and make with the second as much as the sixth hath, which contains four more than the third tripled. Now tell me, my lord, how am I called?"

Virgo lucifera gratiositas.

Ænigma de Nomine.

The answer was intricate enough, yet I left not off, but said:– "Noble and vertuous Lady, may I not obtain one only letter?" "Yea," said she, "that may well be done. "What, then," I proceeded, "may the seventh contain?" "It contains," said she, "as many as there are lords here." With this I easily found her Name, at which she was well pleased, saying that much more should yet be revealed to us. Meantime certain virgins had made themselves ready, and came in with great ceremony. Two youths carried lights before them, one of whom was of jocond countenance, sprightly eyes, and gentile proportion, while the other lookt something angerly, and whatever he would have must be, as I afterwards perceived. Four Virgins followed them; one looked shamefully towards the earth; the second also was a modest, bashful Virgin; the third, as she entered, seemed amazed at somewhat, and, as I understood, she cannot well abide where there is too much mirth. The fourth brought with her certain small wreaths, to manifest her kindness and liberality. After these four came two somewhat more gloriously apparelled; they saluted us courteously. One of them had a gown of skeye-colour, spangled with golden stars: the other's was green, beautified with red and white stripes. On their heads they had thin flying white tiffaties, which did most becomingly adorn them. At last came

60, Sc. quo virgines.

Redduntur pondera choro Virginum.

4 Virgines.

2 Juvenes.

2 Virgines.

78

one alone, wearing a coronet, and rather looking up towards heaven than towards earth. We all took her for the Bride, but were much mistaken, although in honour, riches, and state she much surpassed the bride, and afterwards ruled the whole Wedding. On this occasion we all followed our Virgin, and fell on our knees; howbeit, she shewed herself extreamly humble, offering each her hand, and admonishing us not to be too much surprized at this, which was one of her smallest bounties, but to lift up our eyes to our Creator and acknowledge his Omnipotency, and so proceed in our enterprised course, employing this grace to the praise of God and the good of man. In sum her words were quite different from those of our Virgin, who was somewhat more worldly. They pierced even through my bones and marrow. "Thou," said she further to me, "hast received more than others; see that thou also make a larger return."

The Dutchess.

Ponderum repositio in locum suum.

This to me was a very strange sermon, for as soon as we saw the Virgins with the musick, we imagined we should fall to dancing. Now the Weights stood still in the same place, wherefore the Queen (I yet know not who she was) commanded each Virgin to take up one, but to our Virgin she gave her own, which was the largest, and commanded us to follow behind. Our majesty was then somewhat abated, for I observed that our Virgin was but too good for us, and that we were not so highly reputed as we ourselves were almost willing to phantsie. We were brought into the first Chamber, where our Virgin hung up the Queen's weight, during which an excellent spiritual hymn was sung. There was nothing costly in this room save certain curious little Prayer-Books which should never be missing. In the midst was a pulpit, convenient for prayer, where in the Queen kneeled down, and about her we also were fain to kneel and pray after the Virgin, who read out of a book, that this Wedding might tend to the honour of God, and our own benefit. We then came into the second chamber, where the first Virgin hung up her weight also, and so forward till all the ceremonies were finished, upon which the Queen again presented her hand to every one, and departed with her Virgins. Our president staied awhile with us, but because it had been already two hours night she would then no longer detain us, and, though methought she was glad of our company, she bid us good night, wishing us quiet rest. Our Pages were well instructed, and shewed every man his chamber, staying with

The Dutchess.

Reginæ habitatio.

Supellex.

The Dutchess.

Virgo lucifera discedit cubitum.

Puerorum comitum

us in another pallet, in case we wanted any thing. My chamber was royally furnished with rare tapistries, and hung about with paintings; but above all things I was delighted in my Page, who was so excellently spoken, and experienced in the arts, that he yet spent me another hour, and it was half an hour after three when I fell asleep. This was the first night that I slept in quiet, and yet a scurvy dream would not suffer me to rest, for I was troubled with a Door which I could not get open, though at last I did so. With these phantasies I passed the time, till at length, towards day, I awaked.

Somnium
deportis
difficili.

THE FOURTH DAY.

Autor
longiuscule
dormiens
expergesit.

I still lay in my bed, and leisurely surveighed the noble images and figures about my chamber, during which, on a sudden, I heard the musick of coronets, as if already they had been in procession. My Page skipped out of the bed as if he had been at his wits' end, and looked more like one dead than living. "The rest are already presented to the King," said he. I knew not what else to do but weep outright, and curse my own sloathfulness. I dressed myself, but my Page was ready long before me, and ran out of the chamber to see how affairs might yet stand. He soon returned with the joyful news that the time was not past, only I had over-slept my breakfast, they being unwilling to waken me because of my age, but that now it was time for me to go with him to the Fountain, where most were assembled. With this consolation my spirit returned, wherefore I was soon ready with my habit, and went after the Page to the Fountain in the Garden, where I found that the Lyon, instead of his sword, had a pretty large tablet by him. Having well viewed it, I found that it was taken out of the ancient monuments, and placed here for some especial honour. The inscription was worn with age, and, therefore, I am minded to set it down here, as it is, and give every one leave to consider it.

Jentaculo
privatur.

Leonis
Tabula

HERMES PRINCEPS.

POST TOT ILLATA

GENERI HUMANO DAMNA,

DEI CONSILIO:

ARTISQUE ADMINICULO

MEDICINA SALUBRIS FACTUS

HEIC FLUO.

Bibat ex me qui potest: lavet, qui vult: turbet, qui audet:

BIBITE FRATRES, ET VIVITE.

Scriptura facilis.

This writing might well be read and understood, being easier than any of the rest. After we had washed ourselves out of the Fountain, and every man had taken a draught out of an intirely golden cup, we once more followed the Virgin into the hall, and *Potus.* there put on new apparel, all of cloth of gold gloriously set out *Vestitus.* with flowers. There was also given to everyone another Golden Fleece, set about with pretious stones, and various workmanship according to the utmost skill of each artificer. On it hung a weighty medal of gold, whereupon were figured the sun and moon in opposition, but on the other side stood this poesie:– "The light of the moon shall be as the light of the sun, and the light of the sun shall be seven times brighter than at present." Our former jewels *Clinodiæ.* were laid in a little casket, and committed to one of the waiters. After this the Virgin led us out in our order, where the musitians *Musici.* waited ready at the door, all apparelled in red velvet with white guards. After which a door, that I never before saw open, was unlocked; it opened on the Royal winding-stairs. There the *Accessus ad* Virgin led us, together with the musick, up three hundred sixty- *regis aulam.*

five stairs; we saw nothing but what was of extream costly and artificial workmanship; the further we went, the more glorious still was the furniture, until at the top we came under a painted arch, where the sixty virgins attended us, all richly apparelled.

Laboratorium aronatum 60 Virgines.

As soon as they had bowed to us, and we as well as we could had returned our reverence, the musitians were dispatched away down the winding-stairs, the Door being shut after them. Then a little Bell was told, when in came a beautiful Virgin, who brought every one a wreath of lawrel, but our Virgins had branches given

Virg. Lucif.

them. Meanwhile, a curtain was drawn up, where I saw the King and Queen as they sate in their majesty, and had not the yesterday queen warned me I should have equalled this unspeakable glory to Heaven; for besides that the room glittered of meer gold and pretious stones, the Queen's robes were so made that I was not

Regis et Reginæ gloria.

Virgo lucifera præsentat hospites Regi.

able to behold them. In the meantime the Virgin stept in, and then each of the other virgins, taking one of us by the hand, with most profound reverence presented us to the King. Whereupon the Virgin began thus to speak:– "That to honour your most gratious, royal Majesties, these Lords have adventured hither with peril of body and life, your Majesties have reason to rejoyce, especially since the greatest part are qualified for inlarging your Majesties' dominions, as you will find by a most gratious particular examination of each. Herewith I was desirous thus to have them in humility presented to your Majesties, with most humble suit to discharge me of this my commission, and to take information from each of them concerning my actions and omissions." Hereupon she laid her branch on the ground. It would have been fitting for one of us to have spoken somewhat on this occasion,

Hospites nesciunt respondere. Atlas respondet.

but, seeing we were all troubled with the falling of the uvula, old Atlas stept forward and spoke on the King's behalf:– "Their Royal Majesties most gratiously rejoyce at your arrival, and will that their grace be assured to all. With thy administration, gentle Virgin, they are most gratiously satisfied, and a Royal Reward shall be provided for thee; yet it is their intention that thou shalt this day also continue with them, inasmuch as they have no reason to mistrust thee."

Here the Virgin humbly took up the branch, and we for this first time were to step aside with her. This room was square on the front, five times broader than it was long, but towards the West it

Descriptio labatorii.

Subscellia.

had a great arch like a porch, where stood in circle three glorious

2. Rex &
conjux
senes.

thrones, the middlemost being somewhat higher than the rest. In each throne sate two persons—in the first sate a very antient King with a gray beard, yet his consort was extraordinarily fair and young. In the third throne sate a black King of middle age, and by him a dainty old matron, not crowned, but covered with a vail. But in the middle sate the two young persons, who though they had likewise wreaths of lawrel upon their heads, yet over them hung a large and costly crown. Now albeit they were not at this time so fair as I had before imagined to my self, yet so it was to be. Behind them on a round form sat for the most part antient men, yet none had any sword or other weapon about him. Neither saw I any life-guard but certain Virgins which were with us the day before, and who sate on the sides of the arch. I cannot pass in silence how the little Cupid flew to and again there, but for the most part he hovered about the great crown. Sometimes he seated himself in between the two lovers, somewhat smiling upon them with his bow. Sometimes he made as if he would shoot one of us; in brief, this knave was so full of his waggery, that he would not spare even the little birds, which in multitudes flew up and down the room, but tormented them all he could. The virgins also had their pastimes with him, and when they could catch him it was no easie matter for him to get from them again. Thus this little knave made all the sport and mirth. Before the Queen stood a small but inexpressibly curious altar, wherein lay a book covered with black velvet, only a little overlaid with gold. By this stood a taper in an ivory candlestick, which, although very small, burnt continually, and stood in that manner, that had not Cupid, in sport, now and then puffed upon it, we could not have conceived it to be fire. By this stood a sphere or celestial globe, which of itself turned about. Next this was a small striking-watch, by that a little christal pipe or syphon-fountain, out of which perpetually ran a clear blood-red liquor, and last of all there was a scull or death's head, in which was a white serpent, of such a length, that though she crept circle-wise about the rest of it, yet her taile still remained in one of the eye-holes until her head again entered at the other; so she never stirred from her scull, unless Cupid twitched a little at her, when she slipt in so suddenly that we could not choose but marvel at it. There were hung up and down the room wonderful images, which moved as if alive. Likewise, as we were passing out, there began such marvellous vocal musick that I could not tell whether

Cupide.

Aves.

Supellex in
aula altare

2. Taper.

4. Watch.

6. Scull.
serpent.

Musicæ.

1. Rex senex
Conjux
Juven.

Scomna.
assessores.

Virgines.

1. Book.

3. Sphære.

5. Little
Fountain.

Imagines.

it were performed by the virgins who yet stayed behind, or by the images themselves. We, being for this time satisfied, went thence with our virgins who, the musitians, being already present, *Disceditur ex* led us down the winding stairs, the door being diligently locked *laboratorio* and bolted. As soon as we were come again into the hall, one of the virgins began:– "I wonder, Sister, that you durst adventure yourself amongst so many persons." "My Sister," replyed our *Virgines* president, "I am fearful of none so much as of this man," pointing *jocantur de* at me. This speech went to my heart, for I understood that she *senio autoris.* mocked at my age, and indeed I was the oldest of all; yet she comforted me by promising, that in case I behaved myself well towards her, she would easily rid me of this burden.

Meantime a collation was again brought in, and every one's Virgin seated by him, who well knew how to shorten the time *Convivium* with handsom discourses, but what these and their sports were I *cum virginibus.* dare not blab out of school. Most of the questions were about the *Sermones* arts, whereby I could lightly gather that both young and old were *conviviales.* conversant in the sciences. Still it run in my thoughts how I might become young again, whereupon I was somewhat the sadder. This *Autor mœstus* the Virgin perceived, and, therefore, began:– "I dare lay anything, *ob senio.* if I lye with him to-night, he shall be pleasanter in the morning." *Jocosum* Hereupon they began to laugh, and albeit I blushed all over, I was *solatium* fain to laugh too at my own ill-luck. Now there was one there that *accipit à* had a mind to return my disgrace upon the Virgin, whereupon *a Virgine.* he said:– "I hope not only we but the virgins themselves will bear witness, that our Lady President hath promised herself to *Socio.* be his bed-fellow to-night." "I should be well content with it," replyed the Virgin, "if I had not reason to be afraid of these my sisters; there would be no hold with them should I choose the best and handsomest for myself." "My Sister," presently began *Virg. lucif.* another, "we find hereby that thy high office makes thee not proud, wherefore if by thy permission we might by lot part the Lords here present, thou shouldst, with our goodwill, have such a prerogative." We let this pass for a jest, and began again to discourse together, but our Virgin could not leave tormenting us, and continued:– "My lords, how if we should permit fourtune to decide which of us must be together to-night?" "Well," said *Ludicra* I, "if it may be no otherwise, we cannot refuse such a proffer." *electio una* Now because it was concluded to make this trial after meat, we *dormientium.* resolved to sit no longer at table, so we arose and each walked up and down with his Virgin. "Nay," said the president, "it shall not be so yet, but let us see how fortune will couple us," upon which we were separated. Now first arose a dispute how the business should be carried out, but this was only a premeditated device, for the Virgin instantly proposed that we should mix ourselves in a ring, and that she beginning to count from herself, the seventh was to be content with the following seventh, were it a virgin or man. We were not aware of any craft, and therefore permitted it so to be; but when we thought we had very well mingled ourselves, the Virgins were so subtil that each knew her station before-hand. The president began to reckon, the seventh next her was a Virgin, the third seventh a Virgin likewise, and this continued till, to our amazement, all the Virgins came forth and none of us was hit. Thus we poor wretches remained standing alone, and were forced to confess that we had been handsomely couzened, albeit, whoever had seen us in our order might sooner have expected the sky to fall then that it should never have come to our turn. Herewith our sport was abandoned. In the interim the little wanton Cupid came also in unto us, but because he presented himself on behalf of their Royal Majesties, and deliverd us a health from them out of a golden cup, and was to call our Virgin to the King, withal declaring he could not at this time tarry, we could not sport ourselves with him, so, with a due return of our most humble thanks we let him flye forth again. Now because the mirth began to fall into my consort's feet, and the Virgins were nothing sorry to see it, they lead up a civil dance which I rather

A merry dance.

beheld with pleasure then assisted, for my mercurialists were so ready with their postures, as if they had been long of the trade. After some few dances, our president came in again, and told us how the artists and students had offered themselves to their Royal

Hospites invitantur a virgine Luscif. ad comediam.

Majesties before their departure to act a merry comedy; and if we thought good to be present thereat, and to waite upon their Royal Majesties to the House of the Sun, it would be acceptable to them. Hereupon we returned our humble thanks for the honour vouchsafed us, and most submissively tendered our small service, which the Virgin related, and presently brought word to attend

Processus Regis ad spectandum comediam.

their Royal Majesties in the gallery, whither we were soon led, and staid not long there, for the Royal Procession was just ready, yet without musick. The unknown Queen who was yesterday with us went foremost with a small and costly coronet, apparelled in white satin, and carrying nothing but a small crucifix made of a pearl, and this very day wrought between the young King and his Bride. After her went the six fore-mentioned Virgins in two ranks, carrying the King's jewels belonging to the little altar. Next to these came the three Kings. The Bridegroom was in the midst of them with a plain dress of black sattin, after the Italian mode. He had on a small round black hat, with a little black pointed feather, which he courteously put off to us, thereby to signify his favour towards us. To him we bowed, as we had been before instructed. After the Kings came the three Queens, two whereof were richly habited; she in the middle went likewise all in black, and Cupid held up her train. Intimation was given us to follow, and after us the Virgins, old Atlas bringing up the rear. Through many stately walks we came to the House of the Sun, there next to the King and Queen, upon a richly furnished scaffold, to behold the foreordained comedy. We, though separated, stood on the right hand of the Kings, but the *Statio* Virgins on the left, except those to whom the Royal Ensignes were *spectatorum* committed. To them was allotted a peculiar standing at top of all, but the rest of the attendants were content to stand below between *A Precipuâ* the columns. Now because there are many remarkable passages in *quæ* this Comedy, I will in brief run it over. *agebantur.*

First of all came forth a very antient King with some servants; *Actus 1.* before his throne was brought a little chest, with mention that it was found upon the water. Being opened, there appeared in it a lovely babe, together with certain jewels, and a small parchment sealed, and superscribed to the King. This the King presently opened, and having read it, he wept and declared to his servants how injuriously the King of the Moores had deprived his aunt of her country, and had extinguished all the royal seed even to this infant, with the Daughter of which country he had purposed to match his Son. Hereupon he swore to maintain perpetual enmity with the Moore and his allies, and to revenge this on him. He commanded that the Child should be tenderly nursed, and to make preparations against the Moore. This provision, and the discipline of the young lady (who after she was a little grown up was committed to an ancient tutor), continued all the first act, with many laudable sports beside. In the interlude a Lyon and Griffon were set at one another, and the *Interludium.* Lyon got the victory; this was also a pretty sight.

In the second act, the Moore, a black, treacherous fellow, *Actus 2.* came forth, who having with vexation understood that his murder was discovered, and that a little lady was craftily stollen from him, began to consult how by stratagem he might encounter so powerful an adversary, whereof he was at length advised by certain fugitives who fled to him through famine. So the young lady, contrary to all expectation, fell again into his hands, whom had he not been wonderfully deceived by his own servants, he had like to have slain. Thus this act was concluded with a mervelous triumph of the Moore.

Actus 3.

In the third act a great army on the King's part was raised against the Moore, and put under the conduct of an ancient, valiant knight, who fell into the Moore's country, till he forceably rescued the young Lady from a tower, and apparelled her anew. After this they erected a glorious scaffold and placed her upon it; presently came twelve royal embassadors, amongst whom the Knight made a speech, alledging that the King, his most gracious Lord, had not only heretofore delivered her from death, and caused her to be royally brought up, though she had not behaved herself altogether as became her, but, moreover, had, before others, elected her as a spouse for the young Lord, his Son, most gratiously desiring that the espousals might be really executed in case they would be sworn to his Majesty upon the following articles. Hereupon out of a patent he caused certain glorious conditions to be read; the young Lady took an oath inviolably to observe the same, returning thanks in most seemly sort for so high a grace. Whereupon they began to sing to the praise of God, of the King, and the young Lady, and for this time so departed. In sport, meanwhile, the four

Interludium.

beasts of *Daniel*, as he saw them in the vision, were brought ilk, all which had its certain signification.

Actus 4.

In the fourth act the young Lady was restored to her lost kingdom and crowned, being in this array conducted about the place with extraordinary joy. After various embassadors presented themselves not only to wish her prosperity but also to behold her glory. Yet it was not long that she preserved her integrity, but began to look wantonly about her, and to wink at the embassadors and lords. These her manners were soon known to the Moore, who would by no means neglect such an opportunity; and because her steward had not sufficient regard to her, she was easily blinded with great promises, so that she had no good confidence in her King, but privily submitted herself to the intire disposal of the Moore, who having by her consent gotten her into his hands, he gave her words so long till all her kingdom had subjected itself to him; after which, in the third scene of this act, he caused her to be led forth, stript naked, and then upon a scurvy wooden scaffold bound to a post, well scourged, and at last sentenced to death. This woful spectacle made the eyes of many to run over. Naked as she was, she was cast into prison, there to expect death by poyson, which, however, killed her not, but made her leprous all over. Thus this act was for the most part lamentable. Between they brought forth Nebuchadnezzar's image, which was adorned with all manner of arms on the head, breast, legs, and feet, of which more shall be spoken in the future explication.

Actus 5.   In the fifth act the young King was acquainted with all that had passed between the Moore and his future spouse, who interceded with his father for her, intreating that she might not be left in that condition, and embassadors were dispatched to comfort her, but withal to give her notice of her inconsiderateness. She, nevertheless, would not receive them, but consented to be the Moore's concubine, and the young King was acquainted with it. After this comes a band of fools, each of which brought a cudgel, wherewith they made a great globe of the world, and undid it again, the which was a fine sportive phantsie. *Interludium.*

Actus 6.   In the sixth act, the young King resolved to bid battle to the Moore, which was done, and albeit the Moore was discomfited, yet all held the young King for dead, but he came again to himself, released his spouse, and committed her to his steward and chaplain, the first whereof tormented her mightily, while the priest was so insolently wicked that he would needs be above all, till the same was reported to the young King, who dispatched one to break the neck of the priest's mightiness, and adorn the bride in some measure for the nuptials. After this act a vast artificial elephant was brought in, carrying a great tower with musitians, *Interludium.*
which was well pleasing to all.

Actus 7.   In the last act the bride-groom appeared in such pomp as is not well to be believed. The bride met him in the like solemnity, whereupon all the people cried out–VIVAT SPONSUM, VIVAT SPONSA, so that by this comedy they did withal congratulate our *Comœdorum*
King and Queen in the most stately manner, which pleased them *applansus*
most extraordinary well. At length they made some pastes about *erga Regem*
the stage, till at last they altogether began thus to sing. *et Reginam.*

Cantilena.

This time full of love
Does our joy much approve
Because of the King's Nuptial;
And, therefore, let's sing,
Till from all parts it ring,
Blest be he that granted us all!

II.

The Bride most exquisitely faire,
Whom we attended long with care,
 To him in troth is plighted;
We fully have at length obtain'd
The same for which we did contend
He's happy that's fore-sighted.

III.

Now the parents kind and good
By intreaties are subdued;
Long enough in hold was she mew'd;
So in honour increase
Till Thousands arise
And spring from your own proper blood.

After this thanks were returned, and the comedy was finished with joy to the particular liking of the Royal Persons, who, the evening being already hard by, departed in their fore-mentioned order, we attending them up the winding stairs into the previous hall, where the tables were already richly furnished. This was the first time that we were invited to the King's table. The little altar was placed in the midst of the hall, and the six royal ensignes were laid upon it. The young King behaved himself very gratiously towards us, yet he could not be heartily merry; he discoursed a little with us, yet often sighed, at which the little Cupid only mocked, and played his waggish tricks. The old King and Queen were very serious, but the wife of one of the ancient Kings was gay enough, the cause whereof I understood not. The Royal Persons took up the first table, at the second we only sate; at the third some of the principal Virgins placed themselves. The rest were fain to wait. This was performed with such state and solemn stillness that I am afraid to make many words of it. All

Epilogus.

Hospites invitantur ad cœnam Regis et Reginœ.

Rex Adolesc.

Reges adulti.

Ordo discumbarium.

the Royal Persons, before meat, attired themselves in snow-white

Corona super mensam. glittering garments. Over the table hung the great golden crown, *Ornatus vestium.* the pretious stones whereof, without other light, would have sufficiently illuminated the hall. All the lights were kindled at the small taper upon the altar. The young king frequently sent meat to the white serpent, which caused me to muse. Almost all the prattle at this banquet was made by Cupid, who could not leave us, and *Cupido was the merriest.* me especially, untormented, and was perpetually producing some strange matter. However, there was no considerable mirth, from whence I could imagine some great imminent peril. There was no musick heard, and if we were demanded anything, we were fain to give short answers, and so let it rest. In short, all things *Sermones breves.* had so strange a face that the sweat began to trickle down over my body, and I believe that the stoutest-hearted man would have lost courage.

Supper being almost ended, the young King commanded the book to be reached him from the altar. This he opened and *Oratio Regis adolescentis.* caused it again to be propounded to us by an old man whether we resolved to abide with him in prosperity and adversity, which we having with trembling consented to, he further caused us sadly to be demanded whether we would give him our hands on it, which, when we could fain no reason, was fain so to be. One after another rose and with his own hand writ himself down in this book, after which the little christal fountain was brought near, together with a very small christal glass, out of which all the Royal Persons drank; afterwards it was reached to us, and so forward to all, and *Haustus de silentio.* this was called the Draught of Silence. Hereupon all the Royal Persons presented us their hands, declaring that in case we did not now stick to them we should never hereafter see them, which verily made our eyes run over. But our president engaged herself *Fide jubetur virg. lucif.* and promised largely on our behalf, which gave them satisfaction. Mean time a little bell was tolled, at which all the Royal Persons waxed so mighty bleak that we were ready utterly to despair. They quickly put off their white garments and assumed intirely black *Mors Regulorum.* ones; the whole hall was hung with black velvet, the floor covered with the same, with which also the ceiling was overspread. The tables were also removed, all seated themselves upon the form, and we also had put on black habits. Our president, who was before gone out, comes in again, bearing six black taffeta scarffs, with which she bound the six Royal Persons' eyes, and there were immediately brought in by the servants six covered coffins, which were set down, a low black seat being placed in their midst. Finally, there stept in a cole-black, tall man, who bare in his hand a sharp ax. Now after that the old King had been brought to the seat, his head was instantly whipt off and wrapped in a *Decollatio* black cloth, the blood being received in a great golden goblet, and *Regum.* placed with him in the coffin that stood by, which, being covered, was set aside. Thus it went with the rest, so that I thought it would have come to me too, but as soon as the six Royal Persons were beheaded, the black man retired, another following who just before the door beheaded him also, and brought back his head, *Carnificis.* which, with the ax, was laid in a little chest. This indeed seemed to me a bloody Wedding, but, because I could not tell what the event would be, I was fain to captivate my understanding until I were further resolved. The Virgin, seeing that some of us were *Hospites* faint-hearted and wept, bid us be content, saying:– "The life of *mærent.* these standeth now in your hands, and in case you follow me, this *Solatium.* death shall make many alive."

Herewith she intimated we should go sleep and trouble ourselves no further, for they should have their due right. She bade us all good night, saying that she must watch the dead corps. We then were conducted by our Pages into our lodgings. My Page *Cura* talked with me of sundry matters, and gave me cause enough to *nocturna* admire his understanding, but his intention was to lull me asleep, *mortuorum.* which at last I observed, whereupon I made as though I was fast asleep, but no sleep came to my eyes, and I could not put the *Cubiculum.* beheaded out of my mind. Now my lodging was directly over against the great lake, so that I could look upon it, the windows being nigh the bed. About midnight I espied on the lake a great fire, wherefore I quickly opened the window to see what would *Visio* become of it. Then from far I saw seven ships making forward all *nocturna.* full of lights. Above each of them hovered a flame that passed to and fro, and sometimes descended, so that I could lightly judge that it must needs be the spirits of the beheaded. The ships gently *Cadavera* approached to land, and each had no more than one mariner. *avehuntur* When they were gotten to shore, I espied our Virgin with a torch *trans Lacum.* going towards them, after whom the six covered coffins, together with the little chest, were carried, and each was privily laid in a ship. Wherefore I awaked my Page, who hugely thanked me, for having run much up and down all day, he might quite have over-slept this, though he well knew it. As soon as the coffins were laid in the ships, all the lights were extinguished, and the six flames passed back together over the lake, so that there was but one light for a watch in each ship. There were also some hundreds of watchmen encamped on the shore, who sent the Virgin back again into the Castle, she carefully bolting all up again; so that I could judge that there was nothing more to be done this night.

Autor solus hæc vidit. We again betook ourselves to rest. I only of all my company had a chamber towards the lake and saw this. Then being extream weary I fell asleep in my manifold speculations.

THE FIFTH DAY.

The night was over, and the dear wished-for day broken, when hastily I got me out of bed, more desirous to learn what might insue than that I had sufficiently slept. After I had put on my cloathes, and according to my custom was gone down stairs, it was still too early, and I found nobody else in the hall, wherefore I entreated my Page to lead me a little about the castle, and shew me somewhat that was rare, who now (as always) willing, presently lead me down certain steps underground to a great iron door, on which the following words were fixed in large copper letters:–

Obambulatio antelucana.

VENVS.

These I copied and set down in my table-book. After this door was opened, the Page lead me by the hand through a very dark passage till we came to a little door now only put too, for, as the Page informed me, it was first opened yesterday when the coffins were taken out, and had not since been shut. As soon as we stepped in I espied the most pretious thing that Nature ever created, for this vault had no other light but from certain huge carbuncles. This was the King's Treasury, but the most glorious *Thesaurus* and principal thing was a sepulchre in the middle, so rich that I *Regis.* wondered it was no better guarded, whereunto the Page answered

Descriptio me, that I had good reason to be thankful to my planet, by
sepulchri. whose influence I had now seen certain pieces which no humane eye (except those of the King's family) had ever viewed. This sepulcher was triangular, and had in the middle of it a kettle of polished copper, the rest was of pure gold and pretious stones. In the kettle stood an angel, who held in his arms an unknown tree, whose fruit continually falling into the kettle, turned into water therein, and ran out into three small golden kettles standing by. This little altar was supported by an eagle, an ox, and a lion, which stood on an exceeding costly base. I asked my Page what this might signifie. "Here," said he, "lies buried Lady Venus, that beauty which hath undone many a great man, both in fourtune, honour, blessing, and prosperity"; after which he showed me a copper door in the pavement, saying, "Here, if you please, we *Aliud* may go further down." We descended the steps, where it was *triclinium.* exceeding dark, but the Page immediately opened a little chest in which stood a small ever-burning taper, wherefrom he kindled one of the many torches that lay by. I was mightily terrified and asked how he durst do this. He gave me for answer, "as long as the Royal Persons are still at rest I have nothing to fear." Herewith

Descriptio I espied a rich bed ready made, hung about with curious curtains,
corporis one of which he drew, and I saw the Lady Venus stark naked (for
veneris he heaved up the coverlets too), lying there in such beauty, and a
dormientis. fashion so surprising, that I was almost besides myself, neither do I yet know whether it was a piece thus carved, or an humane corps that lay dead there, for she was altogether immoveable, and yet I durst not touch her. So she was again covered, yet she was still, as it were, in my eye. But I soon espyed behind the bed a tablet on which it was thus written.

I asked my Page concerning this writing, but he laughed, with promise that I should know it too, and, he putting out the torch, we again ascended. Then I better viewed all the little doors, and found that on every corner there burned a small taper of pyrites of which I had before taken no notice, for the fire was so clear that it looked much liker a stone than a taper. From this heat the tree was forced continually to melt, yet it still produced new fruit. "Now, behold," said the Page, "when the tree shall be quite melted down, then shall Lady Venus awake and be the mother of a King." Whilst he was thus speaking, in flew the little Cupid, who at first was somewhat abashed at our presence, but seeing us both look more like the dead then the living, he could not refrain from laughing, and demanded what spirit had brought me thither, whom I with trembling answered, that I had lost my way in the castle, and was by chance come hither, that the Page had likewise been looking up and down for me, and at last lited upon me here, and that I hoped he would not take it amiss. "Nay, then, 'tis well enough yet," said Cupid, "my old busie gransir, but you might lightly have served me a scurvy trick, had you been aware of this door. I must look better to it," and so he put a strong lock on the copper door where we before descended. I thanked God that he lited upon us no sooner; my Page, too, was the more jocond because I had so well helped him at this pinch. "Yet can I not," said Cupid, "let it pass unrevenged that you were so near stumbling upon my dear mother." With

Arboris calor ex facibus.

Mulcta facta hujus obambulationis

94

that he put the point of his dart into one of the little tapers, and heating it somewhat, pricked me with it on the hand, which at that time I little regarded, but was glad that it went so well with us. Meantime my companions were gotten out of bed and were come into the hall, to whom I joyned myself, making as if I were then first risen. After Cupid had carefully made all fast again, he came *Cupido* likewise to us, and would needs have me shew him my hand, *illudit* where he still found a little drop of blood, at which he heartily *autori.*

Mira laughed, and had the rest have a care of me, as I would shortly
Cupidinus end my days. We all wondered how he could be so merry and
lætitia. have no sence of yesterday's sad passages. Our President had *Præsidissæ* meantime made herself ready for a journey, coming in all in black *vestitus* velvet, yet she and her Virgins still bare their branches of lawrel. All *lugubris.* things being in readiness, she bid us first drink somewhat, and then presently prepare for the procession, wherefore we made no long tarrying, but followed her out of the hall into the court, where stood six coffins, and my companions thought no other but that the six Royal Persons lay in them, but I well observed the device, though I knew not what was to be done with these other. By each coffin were eight muffled men. As soon as the musick went, it was so doleful a tune that I was astonished at it, they took up the coffins, and we followed them into the Garden, in the midst of which was erected a wooden edifice, have round about the roof a glorious crown, and standing upon seven columns. Within it were formed six sepulchers; by each of them was a stone, but in the middle it had a round hollow rising stone. In these graves the coffins were quietly, and with many ceremonies, laid; the stones were shoved over them, and they shut fast, but the little chest was to lie in the middle. Herewith were my companions deceived, for they imagined that the dead corps were there. On the top of all was a great flag, having a Phœnix painted on it, perhaps the more to delude us. After the funerals were done, the Virgin, having placed herself upon the midmost stone, made a *Hospites* short oration, exhorting us to be constant to our ingagements, not *vocantur ad* to repine at the pains we must undergo, but be helpful in restoring *labores pro* the buried Royal Persons to life, and therefore, without delay, to *vita Regum.* rise and make a journey with her to the Tower of Olympus, to fetch thence the medicines necessary for this purpose.

This we soon agreed to, and followed her through another little door to the shore, where the seven ships stood empty, and on them all the Virgins stuck up their Laurel branches, and, having distributed us in the six ships, they caused us in God's name to begin our voyage, and looked upon us as long as we were in sight, after which they, with all the watchmen, returned into the Castle. Our ships had each of them a peculiar device; five of them, indeed, had the five regular bodies, each a several one, but mine, in which the Virgin too sate, carried a globe. Thus we sailed on in a singular order, and each had only two mariners. Foremost went the ship *a* in which, as I conceive, the Moor lay. In this were twelve musitians who played excellently well, and its device was a pyramid. Next followed three abreast, *b, c,* and *d,* in which we were disposed; I sate in *c.* Behind these came the two fairest and stateliest ships, *e* and *f,* stuck about with many branches of lawrel, and having no passengers in them; their flags were the sun and moon. But in the rear was only one ship, g, and in this were forty Virgins. Having passed over this lake, we came through a narrow arm into the right sea, where all the sirens, nymphs, and sea-goddesses attended us, and immediately dispatched a sea-nymph unto us to deliver their present of honour to the Wedding.

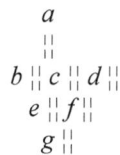

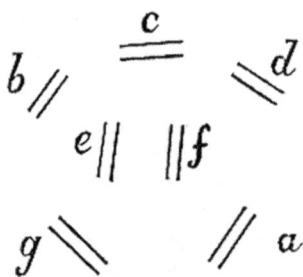

It was a costly, great, set, round, and orient pearl, the like to which hath not at any time been seen, either in ours or in the new world, The Virgins having friendly received it, the nymph intreated that audience might be given to their divertisements, which the Virgin was content to give, and commanded the two great ships to stand into the middle, and to the rest to incompass them in pentagon, after which the nymphs fell into a ring about them, and with a most delicate sweet voice began thus to sing

    I.

> There's nothing better here below
> Than beauteous, noble Love,
> Whereby we like to God do grow,
> And none to grief do move;
> Wherefore let's chant it to the King,
> That all the sea therewith may ring.
> We question, answer you!

96

II.

    What was it that at first us made?
        'Twas Love.
    And what hath grace afresh conveigh'd?
        'Twas Love.
    And whence (pray tell us!) were we born?
        Of Love.
    How came we then again forlorn?
        Sans Love.

III.

    Who was it, say, that us conceived?
        'Twas Love.
    Who suckled, nursed, and relieved?
        'Twas Love.
    What do we to our parents owe?
        'Tis Love.
    Why do they us such kindness show?
        Of Love.

IV.

    Who gets herein the victory?
        'Tis Love.
    Can Love by search obtained be?
        By Love.
    How may a man good works perform?
        Through Love.
    Who into one can two transform?
        'Tis Love.

V.

        Then let our song sound,
        Till its eccho rebound,
         To Love's honour and praise;
        May it ever increase
With our noble Princes, the King and the Queen,
The soul is departed, their body's within.

VI.

> And as long as we live
> God graciously give,
> That as great love and amity
> They bear each other mightily,
> So we, likewise, by love's own flame
> May reconjoyn them once again.

VII.

> Then this annoy Into great joy
> (If many thousand younglings deign)
> Shall change, and ever so remain.

Autori
perplacent
nymphæ et
cantus.

These having, with most admirable concent and melody, finished this song, I no more wondred at Ulisses for stopping the ears of his companions; I seemed to myself the most unhappy man alive that Nature had not made me too so trim a creature. But the Virgin soon dispatched them, and commanded to set sail; wherefore the nymphs, having been presented with a long red scarf *The nymphs* for a gratuity, dispersed themselves in the sea. I was at this time *rewarded.*

Autori desunt
adhunc duo.

sensible that Cupid began to work with me too, which tended little to my credit; but as my giddiness is likely to be nothing beneficial to the reader, I am resolved to let it rest. This was the wound that in the first book I received on my head in a dream. Let every one take warning by me of loitering about Venus' bed, for Cupid can by no means brook it. After some hours, we came within ken of the Tower of Olympus; wherefore the Virgin commanded by *Turris* the discharge of some pieces to give signal of our approach, and *Olympi.* immediately we espyed a great white flag thrust out, and a small gilded pinnace sent forth to meet us, wherein was a very antient

Custos

man, the Warder of the Tower, with certain guards in white, by whom we were friendly received, and conducted to the Tower, which was situated upon an island exactly square,[1] and invironed with a wall so firm and thick that I counted two hundred and sixty *Structura*

Dies.

paces over. On the other side was a fine meadow with certain little gardens, in which grew strange, and to me unknown fruits. There was an inner wall about the Tower which itself was as if seven round towers had been built one by another, yet the middlemost was somewhat higher, and within they all entered one into another. Being come to the gates of the Tower, we were led a little aside on the wall, that so the coffins might be brought in without our notice, but of this the rest knew nothing. We were conducted into the Tower at the very bottom, which was an excellently painted laboratory, where we were fain to beat and wash plants, precious stones, and all sorts of things, extract their juice and essence, put up the same in glasses, and deliver them to be laid up. Our Virgin was so busie with us, and so full of directions, that she knew not how to give us employment enough, so that in this island we were meer drudges till we had atchieved all that was necessary for restoring the beheaded bodies. Meantime, as I afterwards learned, three Virgins were in the first apartment washing the corps with diligence. Having at length almost done our preparation, some broath, with a little draught of wine, was brought us, whereby I observed that we were not here for pleasure. When we had finished our day's work, everyone had a mattress laid on the ground for him, wherewith we were to content ourselves. For my part I was not much troubled with sleep, and walking out into the garden, at length came as far as the wall, where, the heaven being very clear, I could well give away the time in contemplating the stars. By chance I came to a great pair of stone stairs leading to the top of the wall, and because the moon shone very bright, I was so much the more confident, and, going up, looked too a little upon the sea, which was exceeding calm. Thus having good opportunity to consider better of astronomy, I found that this night there would happen such a conjunction of the planets, the like to which was not otherwise suddenly to be observed. Having looked a good while into the sea, and it being just about midnight, I beheld from far the seven Flames passing over sea hitherward, and betakeing themselves to the top of the spire of the tower. This made me somewhat affraid; for as soon as the Flames had settled themselves, the winds rose, and made the sea very tempestuous. The noon also was covered with clouds, and my joy ended with such fear that I had scarce time enough to hit upon the stairs again, and betake myself to the Tower, where I laid me down upon my mattress, and there being in the laboratory a pleasant and gently purling fountain, I fell asleep so much the sooner. And thus this fifth day too was concluded with wonders.

1. Conclave.

Labores hospitum.

Virginum.

Cibus. Potus.

Lectus tenuis.

Autor speculator cælum prosomno.

Footnotes

1. The symbolical representation of the tetrad as a four-square garden, enclosure, house, or city is very common among mystical writers.

THE SIXTH DAY.

Next morning, after we had awaked another, we sate together to discourse what might be the wont of things. Some were of opinion that the corps should all be inlivened again together. Others contradicted this, because the decease of the ancients was not only to restore life but increase too to the young ones. Some imagined that they were not put to death, but that others were beheaded in their stead. Having talked a pretty while, in comes the old man, and first saluting us, looks about to see if all things were ready. We had herein so behaved ourselves that he had no fault to find with our diligence, whereupon he placed all the glasses together, and put them into a case. Presently come certain youths, bringing ladders, roapes, and large wings, which they laid before us and departed. Then the old man began thus:– "My dear Sons, one of these three things must each of you this day constantly bear about with him. It is free for you to make choice of one of them, or to cast lots." We replied that we would choose. "Nay," said he, "let it rather go by lot. Hereupon he made three little schedules, writing on one Ladder, on the second Rope, on the third Wings. These he laid in an hat; each man must draw, and whatever he happened on was to be his. Those who got ropes imagined themselves in the best case; but I chanced on a ladder, which hugely afflicted me, for it was twelve-foot long, pretty weighty, and I must be forced to carry it, whereas the others could handsomely coyle their ropes about them, and as for the wings, the old man joyned them so neatly on to the third sort as if they had grown upon them. Hereupon he turned the cock, and the fountain ran no longer, and we were fain to remove it out of the way. After all things were carried off, he, taking with him the casket and glasses, took leave, and locked the door after him, so we imagined that we had been imprisoned in this Tower; but it was hardly a quarter of an hour before a round hole above was uncovered, where we saw our Virgin, who bad us good morrow, desiring us to come up. They with the wings were instantly through the hole; only they with the ropes were in an evil plight, for as soon as ever one of us was up, he was commanded to draw up the ladder to him. At last each man's rope was hanged on an iron hook, and he climbed up as well as he could, which indeed was not compassed without blisters. When we were all well up, the hole was again

Define ortæ dubiæ opiniones.

Pyrotechnia hospitum laudatur.

Sors.

Ascensus in 2 conclave.

Custos.

Pueri armiferi.

Restis difficultas.

covered, and we were friendly received by the Virgin. This room was the whole breadth of the Tower itself, having six very stately vestries a little raised and reached by three steps. In these we were distributed to pray for the life of the King and Queen. Meanwhile the Virgin went in and out at the little door a till we had done. As soon as our process was absolved, there was brought in through the little door by twelve persons, which were formerly our musitians, a wonderful thing of longish shape, which my companions took to be a fountain, and which was placed in the middle. I well observed that the corps lay in it, for the inner chest was of an oval figure, so large that six persons might well lie therein one by another. After this they again went forth, fetched their instruments, and conducted in our Virgin, with her she-attendants, to a most delicate voice of musick. The Virgin carried a little casket, the rest only branches, *The little* and small lamps or lighted torches, which last were immediately *casket.* given into our hands, and we stood about the fountain in this order.

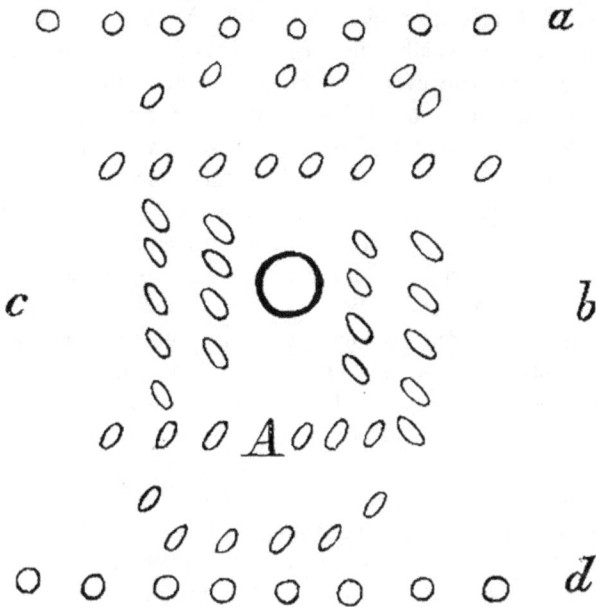

First stood the Virgin *A*, with her attendants in a ring round about, with the lamps and branches *c*. Next stood we with our torches *b*, then the musitians in a long rank; last of all, the rest of the Virgins *d*, in another long rank. Whence the Virgins came, whether they dwelt in the Castle, or were brought in by night, I know not, for their faces were covered with delicate white linnen.

The Virgin opened the casket, in which was a round thing wrapped in a piece of green double taffata. This she laid in the uppermost kettle, and covered it with the lid, which was full of holes, and had besides a rim, on which she poured in some of the water which we had the day before prepared; the fountain began immediately began to run, and through four small pipes to drive into the little kettle. Beneath the undermost kettle were many sharp points, on which the Virgins stuck their lamps, that the heat might come to the kettle and make the water seeth, which, when it began to simper, by many little holes at *a*, fell in upon the bodies, and was so hot that it dissolved them all, and turned them into liquor. What the above-said round wrapt-up thing was, my companions knew not, but I understood that it was the Moor's head, from which

the water conceived so great heat. At *b*, round about the great kettle, there were again many holes, in which they stuck their branches, but whether this was done of necessity or for ceremony I know not. However, these branches were continually sprinkled by the fountain, whence it afterwards dropt somewhat of a deeper yellow into the kettle. This lasted for near two hours, the fountain still running, but more faintly. Meantime the musitians went their way, and we walked up and down in the room, which truly was so made that we had opportunity enough to pass away our time.

There were images, paintings, clock-works, organs, springing fountains, and the like. When it was near the time that the fountain ceased, the Virgin commanded a golden globe to be brought. At the bottom of the fountain was a tap, by which she let out all the matter dissolved by those hot drops (whereof certain quarts were then very red) into the globe. The rest of the water above in the kettle was poured out, and so this fountain was again carried forth. Whether it was opened abroad, or whether anything of the bodies that was useful yet remained, I dare not certainly say, but

the water emptied into the globe was much heavier than six or more of us were able to bear, albeit for its bulk it should have seemed not too heavy for one man. This globe being with much ado gotten out of doors, we again sate alone, but I, perceiving a trampling over head, had an eye to my ladder. After one quarter of an hour, the cover above was lifted, and we commanded to come up, which we did as before, with wings, ladders, and ropes, and it

Ascensus in 3 conclave. did not a little vex me that whereas the Virgins could go up another way, we were fain to take so much toil; yet I could judge there must be some special reason for it, and we must leave somewhat for the old man to do too. The hole being again shut fast, I saw the globe hanging by a strong chain in the middle of the room, in which there was nothing but windows, with a door between every *Descriptio* two, which was covered with a great polished looking-glass. *conclavis.* These windows and looking-glasses were so optically opposed that although the sun, which now shined exceeding bright, beat only upon one door, yet (after the windows towards the sun were *Artif. optica.* opened, and the doors before the looking-glasses drawn aside) in all quarters of the room there was nothing but suns, which by artificial refractions beat upon the whole golden globe hanging in the midst, which, being polished, gave such a lustre that none of us could open our eyes, but were forced to look out at windows till the globe was well heated, and brought to the desired effect. In these mirrors I saw the most wonderful spectacles that ever *Mirac. spec.* nature brought to light, for there were suns in all places, and the globe in the middle shined brighter yet. At length the virgin commanded to shut up the looking-glasses and make fast the windows to let the globe cool a little, wherefore we thought good, since we might now have leisure, to refresh ourselves with a *Prandium* breakfast. This treatment was again right philosophical, and we *philosoph.* had no need to be afraid of intemperance, though we had no want, while the hope of the future joy, with which the virgin continually comforted us, made us so jocond that we regarded not any pains or inconvenience. I can truly say concerning my companions of high quality that their minds never ran after their kitchen or table, but their pleasure was only to attend on this adventurous physic, and hence to contemplate the Creator's wisdom and omnipotency. After our refection we settled ourselves to work, for the globe was sufficiently cooled, which with toil and labour we were to lift off the chain and set upon the floor. The dispute then was how we were to get the globe in sunder, for we were commanded to divide it in the midst. The conclusion was that a sharp-pointed diamond would be best to do it, and when we had thus opened the globe, there was no redness to be seen, but a lovely great snow-white egg, and it mightily rejoyced us that this was so well brought to pass, for the virgin was in perpetual care least the shell might still be too tender. We stood around about this egg as jocond as if we ourselves had laid it, but the Virgin made it presently be carried forth, and departed herself, locking the door behind her. What she did abroad with the egg, or whether it were privately handled, I know not, neither do I believe it. We were again to pause for one quarter of an hour, till the third hole opened, and we, by means of our instruments, came upon the fourth stone or floor. In this room we found a great copper kettle filled with silver sand, which was warmed with a gentle fire, and afterwards the egg was raked up in it, that it might therein come to perfect maturity. This kettle was exactly square. Upon one side stood these two verses writ in great letters–

O. BLI. TO. BIT. MI. LI.
KANT. I. 1 VOLT. BIT. TO. GOLT.

On the second side were these three words–

SANITAS. NIX. HASTA.

The third had but this one word–

F.I.A.T.

But on the hindmost part stood an entire inscription, running thus–

QUOD
Ignis: Aer: Aqua: Terra:
SANCTIS REGUM ET REGINARUM NOSTR:
Cineribus
Eripere non potuerunt.
Fidelis Chymicorum Turba
IN HANC URNAM
Contulit.
Aó

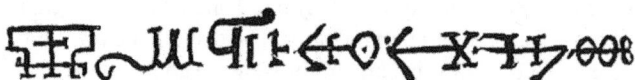

𝍏 𝍖 𝍗 𝍘 𝍙 𝍚 𝍛 𝍜 𝍝

Now, whether the sand or egg were hereby meant I leave the learned to dispute. Our egg, being ready, was taken out, but it needed no cracking, for the Bird soon freed himself, looking very jocond, though bloody and unshapen. We first set him on the warm

Pullus
implumis.

sand, the Virgin commanding that before we gave him anything to eat we should be sure to make him fast, otherwise he would give us all work enough. This being done, food was brought him, *Vincitur.* which surely was nothing but the blood of the beheaded deluted with prepared water, by which the Bird grew so fast under our eye that we well saw why the Virgin gave such warning of him. He bit and scratched so devilishly that, could he have had his will upon any of us, he would soon have dispatched him. Now he was wholly black and wild, wherefore other meat was brought him, perhaps the blood of another of the Royal Persons, whereupon all his black feathers moulted and were replaced by snow-white ones. He was somewhat tamer too, and more tractable, though we did not yet trust him. At the third feeding his feathers began to be so curiously coloured that I never saw the like for beauty. He was *Iridescit.* also exceedingly tame, and behaved himself so friendly with us that, the Virgin consenting, we released him from captivity. "'Tis now reason," she began, "since by your diligence, and our old man's consent, the Bird has attained with his life and the highest perfection, that he be also joyfully consecrated by us." Herewith she commanded to bring in dinner, since the most troublesome part of our work was now over, and it was fit we should begin to enjoy our passed labours. We began to make merry together. Howbeit, we had still our mourning cloaths on, which seemed somewhat reproachful to our mirth. The Virgin was perpetually inquisitive, perhaps to find to which of us her future purpose *Primus* might prove serviceable, but her discourse was, for the most part, *usus ejus.* about Melting, and it pleased her well when any one seemed expert in such compendious manuals as do peculiarly commend an artist. This dinner lasted not above three-quarters of an hour, which we yet, for the most part, spent with our Bird, whom we were fain constantly to feed with his meat, though he continued much at the same growth. After Dinner we were not long suffered to digest our food, for the Virgin, together with the Bird, departed from us, and the fifth room was opened, which we reached after *5. Conclave.* the former manner, and tendred our service. In this room a bath was prepared for our Bird, which was so coloured with a fine *Avis* white powder that it had the appearance of milk. It was cool when *balneum.* the Bird was set into it, and he was mighty well pleased with it, drinking of it, and pleasantly sporting in it. But after it began to heat, by reason of the lamps placed under it, we had enough to

Pascitur sanguine decallatorum

Sanguine alius Regis pascitur.

Liberatur vinculis.

Μεθοδία

do to keep him in the bath. We, therefore, clapt a cover on the kettle, and suffered him to thrust out his head through a hole, till he had lost all his feathers in this bath, and was as smooth as a new-born babe, yet the heat did him no further harm. In this bath the feathers were quite consumed, and the bath was thereby turned into blew. At length we gave the Bird air, who of himself sprung out of the kettle, and was so glitteringly smooth that it was a pleasure to behold him. But because he was still somewhat *Vincitur.* wild, we were fain to put a collar, with a chain, about his neck, and so led him up and down the room. Meantime a strong fire was made under the kettle, and the bath sodden away till it all came to a blew stone, which we took out, and, having pounded it, we *Balneum* ground it on a stone, and finally with this colour painted the Bird's *coquitur in* whole skin over, who then looked much more strangely, for he *lapidem.* was all blew except the head, which remained white. Herewith our work in this story was performed, and we, after the Virgin with her blew Bird was departed from us, were called up a hole to *6. Conclave.* the sixth story, where we were mightily troubled, for in the midst a little altar, every way like that in the King's hall, was placed. Upon it stood the six forementioned particulars, and he himself (the Bird) made the seventh. First of all the little fountain was set before him, out of which he drunk a good draught; afterwards he pecked upon the white serpent till she bled mightily. This blood we received in a golden cup, and poured down the Bird's throat, who was mighty averse from it; then we dipt the serpent's head in the fountain, upon which she again revived, and crept into her death's head, so that I saw her no more for a long time. Meanwhile the sphere turned constantly on until it made the desired conjunction. Immediately the watch struck one, upon which there was going another conjunction. Then the watch struck two. Finally, whilst we were observing the third conjunction, and the same was indicated by the watch, the poor Bird of himself submissively laid down his neck upon the book, and willingly *Avis* suffered his head to be smitten off by one of us, thereto chosen by *decollutur.* lot. Howbeit he yielded not one drop of blood till he was opened on the breast, and then the blood spun out so fresh and clear as if it had been a fountain of rubies. His death went to the heart of us, yet we might well judge. that a naked bird would stand us in little stead. We removed the little altar, and assisted the Virgin to *Avis* burn the body, together with the little tablet hanging by, to ashes, *combursitur*

106

with fire kindled at the little taper, afterwards to cleanse the same several times, and to lay them in a box of cypress wood. Here I cannot conceal what a trick I, with three more, was served. After we had diligently taken up the ashes, the Virgin began to speak thus:– "My Lords, we are here in the sixth room, and have only one more before us, in which our trouble will be at an end, and we shall return home to our castle to awaken our most gratious Lords and Ladies. Now albeit I could heartily wish that all of you had behaved yourselves in such sort that I might have given your commendations to our most renowned King and Queen, and you have obtained a suitable reward, yet because, contrary to my desire, I have found amongst you these four"–pointing at me and three others– "lazy and sluggish labourators, and yet according to my good-will to all, I am not willing to deliver them to condign punishment. However, that such negligence may not remain wholly unpunished, I purpose that they shall be excluded from the future seventh and most glorious action of all the rest, and so they shall incur no further blame from their Royal Majesties."

In what a case we now were I leave others to consider, for the Virgin so well knew how to keep her countenance that the water soon ran over our baskets, and we esteemed ourselves the most unhappy of all men. The Virgin by one of her maids, whereof there were many always at hand, caused the musitians to be fetcht, who were with cornets to blow us out of doors with such scorn and derision that they themselves could hardly sound for laughing. But it did particularly afflict us that the Virgin vehemently laughed at our weeping, and that there might be some amongst our companions who were glad of our misfortune. But it proved otherwise, for as soon as we were come out at the door the musitians bid us be of good cheere, and follow them up the winding staires to the eighth floor under the roof, where we found the old man standing upon a little round furnace. He received us friendly, and heartily congratulated us that we were hereto chosen by the Virgin; but after he had understood the fright we had conceived, his belly was ready to burst with laughing that we had taken such good fortune so hainously. "Hence," said he, "my dear sons, learn that man never knoweth how well God intendeth him." The Virgin also came running in, who, after she had sufficiently laughed at us, emptied her ashes into another vessel, filling hers again with other matter, saying, she must now cast a mist before the other artist's eyes, that we in the mean time should obey the old lord, and not remit our former diligence. Herewith she departed from us into the seventh room, whither she called *7. Conclave.* our companions. What she first did with them I cannot tell, for they were not only most earnestly forbidden to speak of it, but we,

Verus labor by reason of our business, durst not peep on them through the
sub tecto. cieling. Our work was to moisten the ashes with our fore-prepared water till they became like a very thin dough, after which we set the matter over the fire till it was well heated; then we cast it into two little forms or moulds, and so let it cool a little, when we had leisure to look on our companions through certain crevices in the floor. They were busie at a furnace, and each was himself fain to *Labor spurius* blow up the fire with a pipe, till he was ready to lose his breath. *in 7 conclavi.* They imagined they were herein wonderfully preferred before us. This blowing lasted till our old man rouzed us to work again. We opened our little forms, and there appeared two bright and almost

Homunculi transparent little images, a male and a female, the like to which
duo. man's eye never saw, each being but four inches long, and that which most mightily surprised me was that they were not hard, but limber and fleshy as other human bodies; yet had they no life, so that I assuredly believe that Lady Venus' image was made after some such way. These angelically fair babes we laid upon two little sattin cushonets, and beheld them till we were almost besotted upon so exquisite an object. The old lord warned us to forbear, and continually to instil the blood of the bird, which had *Pascuntur* been received in a little golden cup, drop after drop into the *sanguine* mouths of the little images, from whence they apparently *avis.* encreased, becoming according to proportion much more beautiful. They grew so big that we lifted them from the little cushonets, and were fain to lay them upon a long table covered with white velvet. The old man commanded us to cover them up to the breast with a piece of fine white double taffata, which,

Pulcherrimus. because of their unspeakable beauty, almost went against us. Before we had in this manner quite spent the blood, they were in their perfect full growth, having gold-yellow curled hair, and the figure of Venus was nothing to them. But there was not yet any natural warmth or sensibility in them; they were dead figures, yet of a lively and natural colour; and since care was to be taken that they grew not too great, the old man would not permit anything more to be given them, but covered their faces too with the silk, and caused the table to be stuck round about with torches. Let the reader imagine not these lights to have been of necessity, for the old man's intent was that we should not observe when the Soul entred into them, as indeed we should not have taken notice of it, in case I had not twice before seen the flames. However, I permitted the other three to remain in their belief, neither did the old man know that I had seen anything more. Hereupon he bid us sit down on a bench over against the table. The Virgin came in with the musick and all furniture, and carried two curious white garments, the like to which I had never seen in the Castle. I thought no other but that they were meer christal, but they were *Vestiuntur.* gentle and not transparent. These she laid upon a table, and after she had disposed her Virgins upon a bench round about, she and the old man began many leger-de-main tricks about the table, *Spectatores* which were done only to blind. All this was managed under the *luduntur.* roof, which was wonderfully formed, for on the inside it was *Descriptio* arched into seven hemispheres, of which the middlemost was *tecti.* somewhat the highest, and had at top a little round hole, which was shut and was observed by none but myself. After many ceremonies stept in six Virgins, each of which bare a large trumpet, rouled about with a green, glittering, and burning material like a wreath, one of which the old man took, and after he had removed some of the lights at top, and uncovered their faces, he placed one of the trumpets upon the mouth of one of the bodies in such manner that the upper and wider part of it was *Usus* directed towards the fore-mentioned hole. Here my companions *tubarum.* always looked upon the images, but as soon as the foliage or *Forti ex cœlo* wreath about the shank of the trumpet was kindled, I saw the hole *venions.* at top open and a bright stream of fire shoot down the tube and pass into the body, whereupon the hole was again covered, and the trumpet removed. With this device my companions were deluded into imagining that life came to the image by the fire of the foliage, for as soon as he received his Soul he twinckled his eyes though scarcely stirring. The second time he placed another *Homunculi* tube upon its mouth, kindled it again, and the Soul was let down *animati alio* through the tube. This was repeated upon each of them three *transferuntur.* times, after which all the lights were extinguished and carried away. The velvet carpets of the table were cast together over them, and immediately a travelling bed was unlocked and made ready, into which, thus wrapped up, they were born, and, after the carpets were taken off them, neatly laid by each other, where, with the curtains drawn before them, they slept a good while. It was now time for the Virgin to see how the other artists behaved themselves; they were well pleased because they were to work in gold, which is indeed a piece of this art, but not the most principal, necessary, and best. They had too a part of these ashes, so that they imagined that the whole Bird was provided for the sake of gold, and that life must thereby be restored to the deceased. Mean time we sate very still, attending when our married couple would awake, and thus about half an hour was spent. Then the wanton Cupid presented himself, and, after he had saluted us all, flew to them behind the curtain, tormenting them till they waked. This happened to them with very great amazement, for they imagined that they had slept from the hour in which they were beheaded. Cupid, after he had. awaked them, and renewed their acquaintance one with another, stepped aside and permitted them to recruit their strength, mean time playing his tricks with us, and at length he would needs have the musick fetcht to be somewhat the merrier. Not long after the Virgin herself comes, and having most humbly saluted the young King and Queen, who found themselves somewhat faint, and having kissed their hands, she brought them the two fore-mentioned curious garments, which they put on, and so stepped forth. There were already prepared two very curious chaires, wherein they placed themselves, and were by us with most profound reverence congratulated, for which the King in his own person most gratiously returned his thanks, and again re-assured us of all grace. It was already about five of clock, wherefore they could make no longer stay; but as soon as ever the chiefest of their furniture could be laden, we were to attend the young Royal Persons down the stairs, through all doors and watches unto the ship, in which they inbarqued, together with certain Virgins and Cupid, and sailed so swiftly that we soon lost sight of them, yet they were met, as I was informed, by certain stately ships, and in four hours time had made many leagues out at sea. After five of clock the musitians were charged to carry all things back to the ships, and to make themselves ready for the voyage, but because this was somewhat long a doing, the old lord commanded forth a party of his concealed soldiers, who had hitherto been planted in the wall so that we had taken no notice of any of them, whereby I observed that this tower was well guarded

De. 7 concl.

Homunculi excitantur a cupidine.

Fuerunt illi qui decollabantur

Conjuges induunt vestimenta ut se conspiciendos præbeant.

Conjuges vehuntur trans mare.

Musick.

Custos senex

Turris custodita a militibus.

against opposition. These soldiers made quick work of our stuff, so that no more remained to be done but to go to supper. The table being compleatly furnished, the Virgin brings us again to our companions, where we were to carry ourselves as if we had truly been in a lamentable condition, while they were always smiling one upon another, though some of them too simpathized with us.

Custos est inspector. At this supper the old lord was with us, who was a most sharp inspector over us, for none could propound anything so discreetly but that he knew how to confute or amend it, or at least to give some good document upon it. I learned most by this lord, and it *Laus hujus senis.* were good that each would apply himself to him, and take notice of his procedure, for then things would not so often and untowardly

The old man's closets. miscarry. After we had taken our nocturnal refection, the old lord led us into his closets of rarities, dispersed among the bulworks, where we saw such wonderful productions of nature, and other things which man's wit in imitation of nature had invented, that we needed a year sufficiently to survey them. Thus we spent a good part of the night by candle-light. At last, because we were more inclined to sleep then see many rarities, we were lodged in rooms in the wall, where we had not only costly good beds but extraordinary handsome chambers, which made us the more wonder why we were forced the day before to undergo so many hardships. In this chamber I had good rest, and, being for the most part without care, and weary with continual labour, the gentle

Somnium prolixum. rushing of the sea helped me to a sound and sweet sleep, for I continued in one dream from eleven of clock till eight in the morning.

THE SEVENTH DAY.

After eight of clock I awaked, and quickly made myself ready, being desirous to return again into the tower, but the dark passages in the wall were so many that I wandered a good while before I could find the way out. The same happened to the rest, till we all meet in the nethermost vault, and habits intirely yellow were given us, together with our golden fleeces. At that time the Virgin declared to us that we were Knights of the Golden Stone, of which we were before ignorant. After we had made ourselves ready, and taken our breakfast, the old man presented each of us with a medal of gold. On the one side stood these words–

Salutantur equites

Hospites deponunt vestes lugubres. Donantur a sene.

Ars naturæ ministra.

AR. NAT. MI.

On the other these,

Temporis natura filia.

TEM. NA. F.

exhorting us to enterprize nothing beyond and against this token of remembrance. Herewith we went forth to the sea, where our ships lay so richly equipped that it was not well possible but that such brave things must first have been brought thither. The ships were twelve in number, six of ours and six of the old lord's, who caused his to be freighted with well-appointed soldiers. But he betook himself to us in our ship, where we were all together. In the first the musitians seated themselves, of which the old lord had also a great number. They sailed before us to shorten the time. Our flags were the twelve celestial signs, and we sate in Libra. Besids other things our ship had a noble and curious clock which showed us all the minutes. The sea was so calm that it was a singular pleasure to sail, but that which surpassed all was the old man's discourse, who so well knew how to pass away our time with wonderful histories that I could have been content to sail with him all my life long. The ships passed on, and before we had sailed two hours the mariner told us that he saw the whole lake almost covered with ships, by which we conjectured they were come out to meet us, which proved true, for as soon as we were gotten out of the sea into the lake of the forementioned river, there stood in to us five hundred ships, one of which sparkled with gold and pretious stones, and in it sate the King and Queen, with lords,

Navis, 1.

Vexilla 12 sign. Navi autoris libra.

Horolog.

Facundia senis.

Obviatio ex arce.

500 naves.

ladies, and virgins of high birth. As soon as they were well in ken of us the pieces were discharged on both sides, and there was such a din of trumpets, shalms, and kettle-drums, that all the ships upon the sea capered again. As soon as we came near, they brought about our ships together and so made a stand. Old Atlas stepped forth on the King's behalf, making a short but handsom oration, wherein he wellcomed us, and demanded whether the royal Presents were in readiness. The rest of my companions were in an huge amazement whence this King should arise, for they imagined no other but that they must again awaken him. We suffered them to continue in their wonderment, and carried ourselves as if it seemed strange to us too. After Atlas' oration out steps our old man, making somewhat a larger reply, wherein he wished the King and Queen all happiness and increase, after which he delivered a curious small casket, but what was in it I know not. It was committed to the custody of Cupid, who hovered between them both. After the oration they again let off a joyful volle of shot, and so we sailed on a good time together, till we arrived at another shore, near the first gate at which I first entred. At this place there attended a great multitude of the King's family, together with some hundreds of horses. As soon as we were come to shore and disembarqued, the King and Queen presented their hands to all of us, one with another, with singular kindness, and so we were to get up on horseback. Here I desire to have the reader friendly entreated not to interpret the following narration to any vain glory of mine, but to credit me that had there been not a special necessity in it, I could well have concealed the honour which was shewed me. We were all distributed amongst the lords, but our old lord and I, most unworthy, were to ride even with the King, each of us bearing a snow-white ensign with a Red Cross. I indeed was made use of because of my age, for we both had long grey beards and hair. I had besides fastened my tokens round about my hat, of which the young King soon took notice, and demanded if I were he who could at the gate redeem these tokens. I answered yes in the most humble manner, but he laughed on me, saying there henceforth needed no ceremony, I was his Father. Then he asked me wherewith I had redeemed them. I answered, "With Water and Salt," whereupon he wondred who had made me so wise, upon which I grew somewhat more confident, and recounted how it had happened to me with my Bread, the Dove,

Applansus.

Atlanti respondet senex.

Regiis conjugibus donum affert Cupido.

Pater.

Atlas oratione excipit hospices.

Honor delatus autori cum sene equitat juxta Regem.

Tesseras solvit sale et aqua.

and the Raven; he was pleased with it, and said expressly, that it must needs be that God had herein vouchsafed me a singular happiness. Herewith we came to the first gate, where the porter with the blew cloaths waited, bearing in his hand a supplication. As soon as he spied me even with the king, he delivered me the supplication, most humbly beseeching me to mention his ingenuity before me towards the King; so, in the first place, I *Primus custos. Ob, visam venerem factus portitor.* demanded of his majesty what the condition of this porter was, who friendly answered me, that he was a very famous and rare astrologer, always in high regard with the Lord his Father, but having on a time committed a fault against Venus, and beheld her in her bed of rest, this punishment was imposed upon him, that he should so long wait at the gate till some one should release him from thence. I replyed, "May he then be released?" "Yes," said the King, "if anyone can be Found that hath as highly transgressed as himself, he must stand in his stead, and the other shall be free. *Autor ejusdem delicterus traditur à portitore.* This word went to my heart; conscience convinced me that I was the offender, yet I held my peace and delivered the supplication. As soon as the King had read it, he was mightily terrified, so that the Queen, who, with our virgins and that other queen whom I mentioned at the hanging of the weights, rid behind us, asked him what the letter might signifie; but he, putting up the paper, began to discourse of other matters, till in about three hours we came quite to the Castle, where we alighted and waited upon the King *Actus in Arce.* into his hall, who called immediately for the old Atlas to come to him in a little closet, and showed him the writing. Atlas made no long tarrying, but rid out to the porter to take better cognizance of the matter, after which the young King, with his spouse and other Lords, Ladies, and Virgins sate down. Then began our Virgin highly to commend the diligence we had used, and the pains and *Virg. lucif.* labour we had undergone, requesting we might be royally rewarded, and that she henceforward might be permitted to enjoy the benefit of her commission. The old lord stood up too, and attested the truth of all that the Virgin had spoken, and that it was but equity that we should on both parts be contented. Hereupon we were to step out a little; it was concluded that each man should make some possible wish, and were to consider of it till after supper. Meantime the King and Queen, for recreation's sake, *Ludus Regis um Regina.* began to play together. It looked not unlike chesse, only it had other laws, for it was the vertues and vices one against another, where it might be ingeniously observed with what plots the vices lay in wait for the vertues, and how to re-encounter them again. This was so properly and artificially performed that it were to be *Artificios.* wished that we had the like game too. During the game in comes Atlas again, and makes his report in private, yet I blushed all over, for my conscience gave me no rest. The King presented me the *Supplicatio* supplication to read, the contents whereof were to this purpose: *portitoris* First, the writer wished the King prosperity and peace, and that *traditum* his seed might be spread far and wide. Afterwards he remonstrated *autori.* that the time was now come wherein, according to the royal promise, he ought to be released; because Venus was already uncovered by one of his guests, for his observations could not lie to him, and that if his Majesty would please to make strict and diligent enquiry, in case this should not prove to be, he would remain before the gate all the days of his life. Then he humbly sued that, upon peril of body and life, he might be present at this night's supper, being in good hopes to spye out the offender and obtain his wished freedom. This was handsomly indited, and I could well perceive his ingenuity, but it was too sharp for me, and I could well have endured never to have seen it. Casting in my mind whether he might perchance be helped through my wish, I asked the King whether he might not be released some other way, but he replyed no, because there was special consideration in the *Triclinium* business, but for this night we might gratifie his desire, so he sent one forth to fetch him in. Mean time the tables were prepared in a spatious room, in which we had never before been, which was so compleat that it is not possible for me to describe it. Into this we were conducted with singular ceremony. Cupid was not present, *Cupido iratus* for the disgrace which had happened to his mother had somewhat *ob venerem* angered him. In brieff, my offence, and the supplication which *visam ab* had been delivered, were the occasion of much sadness, for the *autore.* *Etiam Rex* King was in perplexity how to make inquisition amongst his *condolet.* guests. He caused the porter himself to make his strict surveigh, and showed himself as pleasant as he was able. Howbeit, at length *Lætitia* they began again to be merry, and to bespeak one another with all *discumbentium.* sorts of recreative, profitable discourses. The treatment and other ceremonies then performed it is not necessary to declare, since it is neither the reader's concern nor serviceable to my design, but all exceeded more in invention than that we were overcharged with drinking. This was the last and noblest meal at which I was present. After the bancket the tables were suddainly taken away, and certain curious chairs placed round in circle, in which we, together with the King and Queen, both their old men, the Ladies and Virgins, were to sit. After this a very handsom Page opened the above mentioned glorious little book, when Atlas, immediately placing himself in the midst, bespoke us to the ensuing purpose:– That his Royal Majesty had not yet committed to oblivion the service we had done him, and therefore by way of retribution had elected each of us Knights of the Golden Stone. That it was, therefore, further necessary not only once again to oblige ourselves towards his Royal Majesty, but to vow upon the following articles, and then His Royal Highness would likewise know how to behave himself towards his high people. Upon which he caused the Page to read over these articles:–

Post cœnam obligantur equites legibus suis.

I. You, my Lords the Knights, shall swear that you will at no time ascribe your order either unto any Devil or Spirit, but only to God, your Creator, and His hand-maid Nature.

II. That you will abominate all whoredom, incontinency, and uncleanness, and not defile your order with such vices.

III. That you, through your talents, will be ready to assist all that are worthy and have need of them.

IV. That you desire not to employ this honour to worldly pride and high authority.

V. That you shall not be willing to live longer than God will have you.

At this last article we could not choose but laugh, and it may well have been placed there for a conceit. Now, being sworn them all by the King's scepter, we were afterwards, with the usual ceremonies, installed Knights, and, amongst other privileges, set over ignorance, poverty, and sickness, to handle them at our pleasure. This was afterwards ratified in a little chappel, whither we were conducted in procession, and thanks returned to God for it. There I also at that time, to the honour of God, hung up my golden fleece and hat, and left them for an eternal memorial. And because every one was to write his name there, I writ thus:–

Privilegia.

Summa Scientia nihil Scire,
Fr. CHRISTIANUS ROSENCREUTZ.
Eques aurei Lapidis.
Anno. 1459.

Others writ differently, each as seemed him good; after which we were again brought into the hall, where, being sate down, we were admonished quickly to bethink ourselves what every one would wish. The King and his party retired into a little closet to give audience to our wishes. Each man was called in severally, so that I cannot speak of any man's proper wish; but I thought nothing could be more praiseworthy than, in honour of my order, to demonstrate some laudable vertue, and found that none at present could be more famous and cost me more trouble than gratitude; *Autor optat* wherefore, not regarding that I might well have wished somewhat *liberationem* more agreeable to myself, I vanquished myself, and concluded, *portitoris e* even with my own peril, to free the porter, my benefactor. *gratitudine.* Being called in, I was first demanded whether, having read the supplication, I had suspected nothing concerning the offendor, upon which I began undauntedly to relate how all the business *Autor reus* had passed, how, through ignorance, I fell into that mistake, and *confitens.* so offered myself to undergo all that I had thereby demerited. The King and the rest of the Lords wondred mightily at so un-hoped for confession, and wished me to step aside a little; and as soon as I was called in again, Atlas declared to me that, although it were grievous to the King's Majesty that I, whom he loved above others, was fallen into such a mischance, yet, because it was not possible for him to transgress his ancient usages, he knew not how else to absolve me but that the other must be at liberty and I placed in his stead; yet he would hope that some other would soon be apprehended, that so I might be able to go home again. However, no release was to be hoped for till the marriage feast *Audit* of his future son. This sentence near cost me my life, and I first *sententiam.* hated myself and my twatling tongue in that I could not hold my peace; yet at last I took courage, and, because I considered there was no remedy, I related how this porter had bestowed a token on me and commended me to the other, by whose assistance I stood upon the scale, and so was made partaker of all the honour and joy already received. And therefore now it was equal that I should *Laus* show myself grateful to my benefactor, and was willing gently to *beneficii* sustain inconvenience for his sake, who had been helpful to me *portitoris.* in coming to so high place; but if by my wish anything might be effected, I wished myself at home again, and that so he by me, as *Laudatur* I by my wish, might be at liberty. Answer was made me, that the *à Rege* wishing stretched not so far, yet it was very pleasing to his Royal

Majesty that I had behaved myself so generously, but he was affraid I might still be ignorant into what a miserable condition I had plunged myself through this curiosity. Hereupon the good man was pronounced free, and I, with a sad heart, was fain to step aside. The rest were called for after me, and came jocundly out *Reliqui læti* again, which was still more to my smart, for I imagined no other but *evadunt.* that I must finish my life under the gate. I had also many pensive

Autor thoughts running in my head as to what I should yet undertake,
melancholiat. and wherewith to spend the time. At length I considered that I was now old, and, according to the course of Nature, had few *Spes. Metus.* more years to live, that this anguish and melancholy life would easily dispatch me, and then my doorkeeping would be at an end,

Solatium. and that by a most happy sleep I might quickly bring myself into the grave. Sometimes it vexed me that I had seen such gallant things, and must be robbed of them; sometimes it rejoyced me that before my end I had been accepted to all joy, and should not be forced so shamefully to depart. Thus this was the last and worst shock that I sustained. During these my cogitations the rest were ready, wherefore, after they had received a good night from the King and Lords, each was conducted into his lodging, but I, most wretched man, had nobody to show me the way, and yet must suffer myself to be tormented. That I might be certain of my future function, I was fain to put on the Ring which the other had worn. Finally, the King exhorted me that, since this was the last *Autor accipit* time I was like to see him in this manner, I should behave myself *annulum.* according to my place, and not against the Order, upon which he took me in his arms and kissed me, all which I understood as if in the morning I must sit at my gate. After they had all spoken friendly to me, and at last presented their hands, committing me

Auter dormit to the divine protection, I was by both the old men – the Lord of
cum atlante & the Tower and Atlas – conducted into a glorious lodging, in which
sene custode stood three beds, and each of us lay in one of them, where we yet
Turris. spent almost two, &c.

Here are wanting about two leaves in quarto, and he (the author hereof), whereas he imagined he must in the morning be door-keeper, returned home.

AZILOTH BOOKS

Aziloth Books publishes a wide range of titles ranging from hard-to-find esoteric books - *Parchment Books* - to classic works on fiction, politics and philosophy - *Cathedral Classics*. Our newest venture is *Aziloth Books Children's Classics*, with vibrant new covers and illustrations to complement some of the world's very best children's tales. All our imprints are offered to the reader at a competitive price and through as many mediums and outlets as possible.

We are committed to excellent book production and strive, whenever possible, to add value to our titles with original images, maps and author introductions. With the premium on space in most modern dwellings, we also endeavour - within the limits of good book design - to make our products as slender as possible, allowing more books to be fitted into a given bookshelf area.

We are a small, approachable company and would love to hear any of your comments and suggestions on our plans, products, or indeed on absolutely anything.

Aziloth Books, Rimey Law, Rookhope, Co. Durham, DL13 2BL, England.
t: 01388-517600 e: info@azilothbooks.com w: www.azilothbooks.com

PARCHMENT BOOKS enshrines the concept of the oneness of all true religious traditions - that "the light shines from many different lanterns". Our list below offers titles from both eastern and western spiritual traditions, including Christian, Judaic, Islamic, Daoist, Hindu and Buddhist mystical texts, as well as books on alchemy, hermeticism, paganism, etc..

By bringing together such spiritual texts, we hope to make esoteric and occult knowledge more readily available to those ready to receive it. We do not publish grimoires or titles pertaining to the left hand path. Titles include:

The Prophet	Khalil Gibran
The Madman: His Parables & Poems	Khalil Gibran
Abandonment to Divine Providence	Jean-Pierre de Caussade
Corpus Hermeticum	G. R. S. Mead (trans.)
The Holy Rule of St Benedict	St. Benedict of Nursia
The Confession of St Patrick	St. Patrick
The Outline of Sanity	G. K. Chesterton
An Outline of Occult Science	Rudolf Steiner
The Dialogue Of St Catherine Of Siena	St. Catherine of Siena
*Esoteric Christianity; Thought-Forms**	Annie Besant
The Teachings of Zoroaster	Shapurji A. Kapadia
The Spiritual Exercises of St. Ignatius	St. Ignatius of Loyola
Daemonologie	King James of England
A Dweller on Two Planets	Phylos the Thibetan
*Bushido**	Nitobe Inazo
The Interior Castle	St. Teresa of Avila
*Songs of Innocence & Experience**	William Blake
The Secret of the Rosary	St. Louis Marie de Montfort
From Ritual to Romance	Jessie L. Weston
The God of the Witches	Margaret Murray
Kundalini – an occult experience	George S. Arundale
The Kingdom of God is Within You	Leo Tolstoy
The Trial and Death of Socrates	Plato
A Textbook of Theosophy	Charles W. Leadbetter
Chuang Tzu: Daoist Teachings	Chuang Tzu
Practical Mysticism	Evelyn Underhill
Tao Te Ching (Lao Tzu's 'Book of the Way')	Tzu, Lao
The Most Holy Trinosophia	Le Comte de St.-Germain
Tertium Organum	P. D. Ouspensky
Totem and Taboo	Sigmund Freud
The Kebra Negast	E. A. Wallis Budge
Esoteric Buddhism	Alfred Percy Sinnett
Demian: the story of a youth	Hermann Hesse
Religio Medici	Thomas Browne
The Jefferson Bible	Thomas Jefferson
The Dhammapada	W. Wagiswara & K. Saunders

* with colour illustrations
Obtainable at all good online and local bookstores.

CATHEDRAL CLASSICS hosts an array of classic literature, from erudite ancient tomes to avant-garde, twentieth-century masterpieces, all of which deserve a place in your home. All the world's great novelists are here, Jane Austen, Dickens, Conrad, Arthur Machen and Henry James, brushing shoulders with such disparate luminaries as Sun Tzu, Marcus Aurelius, Kipling, Friedrich Nietzsche, Machiavelli, and Omar Khayam. A small selection is detailed below:

Frankenstein	Mary Shelley
Herland; With Her in Ourland	Charlotte Perkins Gilman
The Time Machine; The Invisible Man	H. G. Wells
Three Men in a Boat	Jerome K Jerome
The Rubaiyat of Omar Khayyam	Omar Khayyam
A Study in Scarlet	Arthur Conan Doyle
The Sign of the Four	Arthur Conan Doyle
The Picture of Dorian Gray	Oscar Wilde
Flatland	Edwin A. Abbott
The Coming Race	Bulwer Lytton
The Adventures of Sherlock Holmes	Arthur Conan Doyle
The Great God Pan	Arthur Machen
Beyond Good and Evil	Friedrich Nietzsche
England, My England	D. H. Lawrence
The Castle of Otranto	Horace Walpole
Self-Reliance, & Other Essays (series1&2)	Ralph W. Emmerson
The Art of War	Sun Tzu
A Shepherd's Life	W. H. Hudson
The Double	Fyodor Dostoyevsky
To the Lighthouse; Mrs Dalloway	Virginia Woolf
The Sorrows of Young Werther	Johann W. Goethe
Leaves of Grass - 1855 edition	Walt Whitman
Analects	Confucius
Beowulf	Anonymous
Plain Tales From The Hills	Rudyard Kipling
The Subjection of Women	John Stuart Mill
The Rights of Man	Thomas Paine
Progress and Poverty	Henry George
Captain Blood	Rafael Sabatini
Captains Courageous	Rudyard Kipling
The Meditations of Marcus Aurelius	Marcus Aurelius
The Social Contract	Jean Jacques Rousseau
War is a Racket	Smedley D. Butler
The Dead	James Joyce
The Old Wives' Tale	Arnold Bennett
Letters Concerning the English Nation	Voltaire
Portrait of the Artist As a Young Man	James Joyce
Coningsby	Benjamin Disraeli

Obtainable at all good online and local bookstores.
View Aziloth Books' full list at: www.azilothbooks.com

View Aziloth Books' full list at: www.azilothbooks.com

Aziloth Books is passionate about bringing the very best in children's classics fiction to the next generation of book-lovers. We believe in the transforming power of children's books to encourage a life-long love of reading, and publish only the best authors and illustrators. With its original design and outstanding quality, our highly successful list has something to suit every age and interest. Titles include:

The Railway Children	Edith Nesbit
Anne of Green Gables	Lucy Maud Montgomery
What Katy Did	Susan Coolidge
Puck of Pook's Hill	Rudyard Kipling
The Jungle Books	Rudyard Kipling
Just So Stories	Rudyard Kipling
Alice Through the Looking Glass	Charles Dodgson
Alice's Adventures in Wonderland*	Charles Dodgson
Black Beauty	Anna Sewell
The War of the Worlds	H. G Wells
The Time Machine	H. G .Wells
The Sleeper Awakes	H. G. Wells
The Invisible Man	H. G. Wells
The Lost World	Sir Arthur Conan Doyle
Gulliver's Travels*	Jonathan Swift
Catriona (David Balfour)	Robert Louis Stevenson
The Water Babies	Charles Kingsley
The First Men in the Moon	Jules Verne
The Secret Garden	Frances Hodgson Burnett
A Little Princess	Frances Hodgson Burnett
Peter Pan*	J. M. Barrie
The Song of Hiawatha*	Henry W. Longfellow
Tales from Shakespeare	Charles and Mary Lamb
The Wonderful Wizard of Oz	L. Frank Baum
The Complete Grimm's Fairy Tales	Jacob & Wilhelm Grimm
The Wind in the Willows*	Kenneth Grahame

*with colour illustrations

Obtainable at all good online and local bookstores.
View Aziloth Books' full list at: www.azilothbooks.com

www.ingramcontent.com/pod-product-compliance
Lightning Source LLC
LaVergne TN
LVHW051135080426
835510LV00018B/2417